Lent with Bishop Morneau

Bishop Robert F. Morneau

Foreword by Wendy Wright

LITURGICAL PRESS
Collegeville, Minnesota

www.litpress.org

Nihil Obstat: Rev. Robert C. Harren, J.C.L., *Censor deputatus.*

Imprimatur: ✝ Most Rev. John F. Kinney, J.C.D., D.D., Bishop of St. Cloud, Minnesota, April 18, 2008.

Cover design by David Manahan, OSB. Illustration courtesy of Saint John's Abbey.

1   2   3   4   5   6   7   8   9

Library of Congress Cataloging-in-Publication Data

Morneau, Robert F., 1938–
    Lent with Bishop Morneau / Robert F. Morneau ; foreword by Wendy Wright.
    p. cm.
    ISBN 978-0-8146-1870-7 (pbk.)
    1. Lent—Meditations.   2. Devotional calendars—Catholic Church.
3. Catholic Church—Prayers and devotions.   I. Title.

    BX2170.L4M685   2008
    242'.34—dc22   2008011181

Contents

Foreword   ix

Introduction   xi

❧✝❧

Ash Wednesday
Righteous Deeds   1

Thursday after Ash Wednesday
Fundamental Option: Life or Death   2

Friday after Ash Wednesday
Fasting   4

Saturday after Ash Wednesday
Health Care Plan   6

First Sunday of Lent—A
The "If " Question   8

First Sunday of Lent—B
Lent: A Serious Season   10

First Sunday of Lent—C
Lead Us Not into Temptation   11

Monday of the First Week of Lent
The Right or the Left?   13

Tuesday of the First Week of Lent
Teach Us How to Pray   15

Wednesday of the First Week of Lent
Profitable Preaching   16

Thursday of the First Week of Lent
Asking, Seeking, Knocking   18

Friday of the First Week of Lent
Reconciliation: God's Plan   19

Saturday of the First Week of Lent
The Impossible Commandment?   21

Second Sunday of Lent—A
Do Not Be Afraid!   23

Second Sunday of Lent—B
The Mountain Experience   25

Second Sunday of Lent—C
Friendship, Faith, Holiness   26

Monday of the Second Week of Lent
The Measuring Cup   28

Tuesday of the Second Week of Lent
Humble Service   30

Wednesday of the Second Week of Lent
Authority: Servant Leadership   31

Thursday of the Second Week of Lent
Friendly Persuasion   33

Friday of the Second Week of Lent
Beatings, Killings, Stonings   34

Saturday of the Second Week of Lent
Lost and Found   36

Third Sunday of Lent—A
Living Water   38

Third Sunday of Lent—B
Good Old Human Nature   39

Third Sunday of Lent—C
Bearing Fruit   41

Monday of the Third Week of Lent
Speaking of Rivers   42

Tuesday of the Third Week of Lent
A God of Extravagance   44

Wednesday of the Third Week of Lent
The Law, the Prophets, the Christ   45

Thursday of the Third Week of Lent
Demons   47

Friday of the Third Week of Lent
Loving Unreservedly   48

Saturday of the Third Week of Lent
Humility: The Divine Achilles Tendon   50

Fourth Sunday of Lent—A
The Gift of Sight   52

Fourth Sunday of Lent—B
A God of Love and Mercy   53

Fourth Sunday of Lent—C
The Ministry of Reconciliation   55

Monday of the Fourth Week of Lent
The Grace of Seeing   56

Tuesday of the Fourth Week of Lent
The Healing Ministry   58

Wednesday of the Fourth Week of Lent
The Works of God   59

Thursday of the Fourth Week of Lent
Moses: The Lawyer   61

Friday of the Fourth Week of Lent
In Cold Blood   62

Saturday of the Fourth Week of Lent
More than Eloquence 64

Fifth Sunday of Lent—A
Troubled in Spirit 66

Fifth Sunday of Lent—B
God's Law 67

Fifth Sunday of Lent—C
Justice and Mercy 69

Monday of the Fifth Week of Lent
Knowing Christ Jesus 70

Tuesday of the Fifth Week of Lent
Above Things/Below Things 72

Wednesday of the Fifth Week of Lent
Presence! Truth! Freedom! 73

Thursday of the Fifth Week of Lent
The Jesus Question 75

Friday of the Fifth Week of Lent
Our Life's Work 76

Saturday of the Fifth Week of Lent
The Dignity of All 78

Palm Sunday of the Lord's Passion—A, B, C
The Road of Suffering 80

Monday of Holy Week
Table Fellowship 81

Tuesday of Holy Week
A Troubled Jesus 83

Wednesday of Holy Week
The Tragedy of the Traitor 84

Holy Thursday Evening
  The Towel and the Table   86

Good Friday of the Lord's Passion
  A Suffering God   87

Holy Saturday Night: The Easter Vigil
  All These Things   89

Easter Sunday: The Resurrection of the Lord
  Jesus: Present and Manifest   91

February 22: The Chair of Peter, Apostle
  The Keys of the Kingdom   93

March 19: Joseph, Husband of the Blessed Virgin
  An Upright Man   94

March 25: Annunciation of the Lord
  The Kinswoman Elizabeth   96

References   98

Foreword

When my children were in junior high school, each late winter/ early spring they would come home with stories about their, to them, rather intimidating eighth grade parochial school teacher. Apparently she was in the habit of countering her chocolate "addiction" with a program of serious Lenten abstinence. "You can always tell it's Lent," they would moan, "Mrs. B. is so grouchy!" I cannot vouch for the veracity of this school yard tale; it may be as much urban legend as fact. But it highlights a rather typical Catholic perception of the Lenten season: Lent is about giving up something. Secondarily it may be seen as a practice of discipline, it being a salutary thing to have to abstain from or forgo or do without in a culture saturated with a sense of instant gratification. Of course, voluntarily giving something up and discipline can be very good things. But Lent is a good deal more than that.

First off, in Lent we are invited to become intimate once again with the harrowing and astonishing story of Jesus' passion and, in the process, with the salvific implications of that story. Lent is about orienting ourselves to the great Christian mystery of Easter. On another level, we are invited to enter into the story, not simply as a tale told long ago but as a present, personal experience. We, like Jesus, are invited to die and rise again. The forty days are therefore a season of preparation, a set-aside time for self-examination, for making space, as it were, in our hearts and minds and lives for a deepening realization of the hope to which we are called. The Scriptures trumpet this for us on Ash Wednesday as the season opens and God is heard to proclaim through the prophet Joel: "Return to me with your whole heart, with fasting, and weeping, and mourning; Rend your hearts, not your garments, and return to the LORD, your God" (Joel 2:12-13a). What is in the way, we need to ask, what blocks us from being fully the people God intends us to be? Lent is also a time given to us to examine our choices. We are placed squarely in that arena on the first Sunday when we stand with Jesus in the desert wilderness and face the temptations in our own lives. Satan tempted Jesus with power, prestige, and wealth. What do we face? In what ways are we un-free? Lent is a season for transformation.

As I have spent time with *Lent with Bishop Morneau* I especially appreciate the manner in which he brings out the rich and multifaceted dimensions of this season in very contemporary yet theologically grounded terms. Bishop Morneau gifts us with his own educated and deeply considered faith, but he also brings to us the wise insights of the many authors with whom he is intimately familiar. With him, Lent is illuminated by classic spiritual writers such as Saints John of the Cross and Teresa of Avila, poets such as Shakespeare and Gerald Manley Hopkins, and seekers of justice and reconciliation such as Nelson Mandela. But mostly, the bishop brings us closer into relationship with the astonishing mystery of the God who loves us and seeks our love in return. Yes, Lent with the bishop is challenging. We meet Jesus, the Master of Paradox, who "knows our dark side," and calls us into the light. We confront our fears, dig deep into our failure to respond to God's invitation. We are asked to rethink our cherished assumptions and reexamine the choices we habitually make. Yes, Lent with Bishop Morneau is challenging. But it is also transformative, for throughout we are aware of the height, breadth, depth, and length of the Love that draws us constantly into the fullness of life.

Wendy M. Wright, PhD
Professor of Theology
Creighton University

Introduction

Darkness shrouds our human journey. Thus we stand in need of God's radiant light, lest we go astray. God's word, which Lent invites us to prayerfully and resolutely reflect upon, is that lamp unto our feet and light for our path (Ps 119:105).

God's word calls us to many things: to pray, fast, and give alms; to forgive as we are forgiven; to bear one another's burden; to welcome the stranger, shelter the homeless, clothe the naked; to rejoice in the Lord always; to bear fruit, fruit that will last. To answer these calls we must turn away from sin, seek repentance, and trust that God's Spirit will guide us on the road to peace.

Mother Teresa committed her life to God's will and to following Jesus in his profound poverty. This "saint of Calcutta" experienced the dark night of the soul, struggled with her vocation within a vocation, and fought vigorously to embrace absolute poverty. Mother Teresa lived God's word. Her intense prayer and dedicated ministry prepared her well to celebrate the Easter mysteries.

We do well in following Mother Teresa's example, in paying attention to the fundamentals of the spiritual life: attention, adherence, and abandonment to God's will. That is impossible on our own, but the same gift of Jesus' Spirit that empowered Mother Teresa also empowers us to hear and live God's word no matter how demanding.

Lent invites us to concentrate in a special way on the spiritual life as we prepare to celebrate our life in Christ more fully, more intimately, and more authentically. The Easter mysteries provide the light we need in this dark world. It is in the shadow of the cross and in the light of the resurrection that we come to know our true identity and the meaning of life.

Fortunately, we do not travel alone. This book serves as a companion on our Lenten journey. It is an invitation to ponder a short passage from God's word each day, share in a reflection, consider several questions, then close with a short prayer. The goal is listening and responding to God.

As we pray in one of the Lenten prefaces: "Each year you give us this joyful season when we prepare to celebrate the paschal mystery with mind and heart renewed. You give us a spirit of loving reverence for you, our Father, of willing service to our neighbor." Blessed Lent.

Righteous Deeds

Readings: Joel 2:12-18; 2 Cor 5:20–6:2; Matt 6:1-6, 16-18

Scripture:
[Jesus said to his disciples:] "[But] take care not to perform righteous deeds in order that people may see them; otherwise, you will have no recompense from your heavenly Father." (Matt 6:1)

Reflection: Righteous deeds are deeds that are "right," that is, actions that respect relationships and enhance them. Three specific righteous deeds are mentioned in our gospel passage: giving alms, praying, and fasting. The first righteous deed of giving and serving others fosters our relationship with our sisters and brothers. Prayer, the dialogue between God and humankind, is a righteous deed that deepens our life of grace. And fasting, the discipline of having control over our own house, means that we are serious about the spiritual freedom that opens our minds and hearts to God's will. It, too, is a righteous deed.

But doing these deeds, important as they are, is not sufficient. Besides the "doing" we are challenged to "do" them in the right way. Here is the land of motivation. We are to pray, fast, and be generous out of love, love for God, love for our own dignity, and love for others. Fasting with a gloomy face, giving alms to receive the praise of others, and praying loudly on street corners just doesn't cut it in the eyes of Jesus. Righteous deeds are done before the Father's face in response to what the Father asks of us.

Saint Paul in his second letter to the Corinthians takes us a step deeper: "For our sake he [God] made him [Jesus] to be sin who did not know sin, so that we might become the righteousness of God in him" (2 Cor 5:21). "Doing" the right thing (praying, fasting, sharing) in the right way leads to "being" righteous. All

1

this is possible because Jesus lives within us and shares with us the Spirit of righteousness. Our call, arising out of baptism, is to become God-like:

> For gracious and merciful is he,
> slow to anger, rich in kindness,
> and relenting in punishment. (Joel 2:13b)

Questions: What do you understand by "righteousness"? Name experiences in your life when you did the "right" thing in the wrong way. What is the connection between "doing" and "being"?

Prayer: Lord God, as we begin this season of Lent, give us the wisdom to understand what you ask of us and the courage to do your will joyfully. You have called each of us into a love relationship with you and to have concern for others. Send your Spirit into our hearts that we will do the right thing in the right way. May we, throughout these forty days, become more and more like you.

Thursday after Ash Wednesday ▬▬▬▬▬

Fundamental Option: Life or Death

Readings: Deut 30:15-20; Luke 9:22-25

Scripture:
I have set before you life and death, the blessing and the curse. Choose life, then, that you and your descendants may live, by loving the LORD, your God, heeding his voice, and holding fast to him. (Deut 30:19b-20a)

Reflection: Moral theologians talk about a fundamental option, that basic orientation that people make toward life or death. Although Moses never went to a theological institution, he understood well that everyone and every nation must choose and that choice is ultimately very limited: life or death! Oh, yes, there are gray areas in which a single choice involves both realities of enhancement and diminishment of life at the same time but, in the end, the fundamental option remains and must be made.

Jesus, the new Moses, sets before His disciples and the crowds an option: save life or lose it. But Jesus, the master of paradox, attempts to help us understand that it is precisely in dying to our selfishness that we rise to new life. Death and life commingle here, and they meet at the foot of the cross. No cross, no resurrection! No death, no life! No surprise that many walked away and even the disciples were befuddled.

Conventional wisdom would have us believe that we can have our cake and eat it too. Certain national movements would have us believe that the taking of innocent human life can be justified. People in the pro-choice camp see no contradiction in the destruction of an infant in the womb and being for human rights. Would that the words of Moses might be heard up and down the land: "Here, then, I have today set before you life and prosperity, death and doom" (Deut 30:15).

Saint Thérèse of Lisieux (1873–97), in writing her autobiography, tells of fundamental option. She writes: "My God, I choose all! I don't want to be a *saint by halves*, I'm not afraid to suffer for You, I fear only one thing: to keep my *own will*; so take it, for '*I choose all*' that you will!"

Lent is a season in which we have the opportunity to step back and look at our past choices and what we are presently choosing. In the end the choices are quite limited: life or death, God's will or our own.

Questions: What do you understand by the term "fundamental option"? In what sense are Moses and Jesus speaking about the same thing? Review your attitudes and behaviors. Which ones are life-giving, which ones are death-dealing?

Prayer: God of life, strengthen our will to choose life. Too often we have failed to be life-givers. Whether through negligence or laziness, we have not expended the energy you have given us to further your kingdom of life, love, and light. May this Lenten season be filled with your grace; may we do whatever is pleasing to you.

Friday after Ash Wednesday

Fasting

Readings: Isa 58:1-9a; Matt 9:14-15

Scripture:
This, rather, is the fasting that I wish:
   releasing those bound unjustly,
   untying the thongs of the yoke;
Setting free the oppressed,
   breaking every yoke. (Isa 58:6)

Reflection: Shakespeare's famous "To be or not to be" raises the question of the meaning of existence. On a lesser note, but one not insignificant, we hear a scriptural question: "To fast or not to fast?"

Discipline and asceticism may not seem as important as whether one wants to live or die. Yet, the whole issue of fasting is a matter of the quality of one's life. Where discipline is wanting, be it physical, psychological, or spiritual, growth is greatly impeded if not totally thwarted. Dissipation of one's energies in all kinds of directions means a wasted life, one that can never mature.

The common sense of the gospel reminds us that there is a time to fast and a time to celebrate. Wearing sackcloth and ashes to a wedding is inappropriate. But once the celebration is over and we return to the routine of ordinary days, then a healthy asceticism must kick in if we are to live life to the full.

Why fast? One reason is for the sake of liberation. If we are "hooked" on any substance, be it tobacco, alcohol, or fear, our choices become very limited. Asceticism frees us to make healthy decisions. A second reason to deny ourselves is to witness to our culture that many "things" are unnecessary for happiness and peace. And third, fasting and asceticism help us to identify with those who are poor and deprived. By forgoing some of the comforts of life, we enter into a kind of solidarity with those less fortunate than we.

"To fast or not to fast?" This is not really an option for a disciple of Jesus. But we must discern its proper time. Once that determination is made, then we must act on that clarity and have the courage to follow God's call.

Questions: What role does fasting play in your life? Which of the three reasons for fasting makes most sense to you? In what areas of your life are you "unfree"? What is the connection between prayer and fasting?

Prayer: Lord Jesus, you invite us during this Lenten season to journey with you and to share more deeply in your life. You call us to a type of fasting that gives life to us and to others. Help us to discern your call so that we and others may come to fullness of life. Come, Lord Jesus, come.

Saturday after Ash Wednesday

Health Care Plan

Readings: Isa 58:9b-14; Luke 5:27-32

Scripture:
[Jesus said . . .], "Those who are healthy do not need a physician, but the sick do. I have not come to call the righteous to repentance but sinners." (Luke 5:31-32)

Reflection: Jesus is deeply concerned with health care. Time and time again we witness his healing art, be it a physical cure of a leper, a psychological healing in driving out demons, or a restoration of spiritual health through the forgiveness of sin. Jesus wants us to be fully alive; sickness and death are forces he came to conquer.

So what is Jesus' health care plan? Two things seem evident: compassion and mercy. Jesus felt deeply the anguish of the human heart. In gazing upon Levi at the customs post our Lord saw someone who had gifts that were not being used. In calling Levi to discipleship, Jesus opened up for Levi a whole new world, one in which generosity and not greed would predominate. Immediately Levi responded by throwing a banquet and inviting his friends to meet the person who changed his life. Jesus' compassion brought healing to Levi and so many others.

Mercy is needed if we are to be spiritually healthy. The gospel is clear: We have all sinned. No exception here. Just as no one is ever 100 percent physically healthy, so too with our souls. There is gap between what God asks of us and what we are and do. That gap is called guilt and shame. Jesus came to heal us of those parasites through the gift of divine mercy. By calling us to repentance, the Lord opens our hearts to receive the Father's ubiquitous mercy.

The American essayist Ralph Waldo Emerson hit the nail on the head: "The first wealth is health." Not just physical, though that is of supreme importance, but psychological and spiritual. Jesus is the divine physician who came to give us the fullness of life.

Questions: What is the quality of your health? In what ways have you experienced the healing power of Jesus' compassion and mercy? Does your personal health plan include the sacrament of reconciliation?

Prayer: Lord Jesus, just as you called Levi to follow you, so too do you call us. Help us to leave behind whatever blocks us from doing the Father's will. Heal us of our greed, pride, and anger. Grant us the fullness of life through the gift of your Holy Spirit. Teach us the way of repentance so that we might once again know your peace and joy.

First Sunday of Lent—A

The "If" Question

Readings: Gen 2:7-9; 3:1-7; Rom 5:12-19; Matt 4:1-11

Scripture:
The tempter approached and said to him, "If you are the Son of God, command that these stones become loaves of bread." (Matt 4:3)

Reflection: Back in 1873, Phoebe Knapp wrote a melody and asked a friend of hers, Fanny Crosby, what the melody said. Fanny replied: "Blessed assurance, Jesus is mine!" This melody and the lyrics were used at the beginning and end of the Academy Award-winning movie *Places in the Heart* (1984).

Here are the words of the whole first stanza: "Blessed assurance, Jesus is mine! / O what a foretaste of glory divine! / Heir of salvation, purchase of God, / Born of His Spirit, washed in His Blood." One can feel the confidence in these words; indeed, one can feel the blessed assurance. There is no "if" here because of the deep faith put in the person of Jesus and his gift of salvation.

Yet, Phoebe Knapp and Fanny Crosby, like all pilgrim people, had to struggle at times with the "if" question. Are we truly the daughters and sons of a loving God? Are we redeemed in the Blood of Christ and born of the Spirit. "If" this is true, why are our lives so often shallow and filled with doubt?

Jesus took upon himself our human nature. From the inside he experienced the pain and struggles of this human journey. Part of that struggle was doubt and, upon the cross, he heard these fate-filled words: "If you are the Son of God, come down from the cross." So, too, at the beginning of his ministry, he had to respond to the "if" question of his identity.

The hymn "Blessed Assurance" contains other phrases that express deep faith: "Echoes of mercy, whispers of love . . . Filled with His goodness, lost in His love." During this season of Lent, we pray that we might experience more deeply God's mercy, goodness, and love. Despite our weaknesses and sins, we are invited to put the "if" questions into the lap of God and let him fill us with the assurance, the blessed assurance, of divine grace.

At the end of the movie *Places in the Heart*, there is a reconciliation scene in which people are receiving Communion. The last to receive are the murdered sheriff and his assailant, both dead for some time. They are shown to be in the church with the "living" and receiving Communion as well. It is wonderful reference to the communion of saints.

The question that was not asked but could be felt was: Did all those people have the blessed assurance of God's love and mercy, or did they, even during the reception of the Communion, struggle with the "if" question? We probably know the answer.

Questions: What assurances do you have of God's love and mercy? What are the "ifs" in your life? If God's love is unconditional, how do you deal with the temptation that is conditional, that is, "if" I do this, "then" God will love me?

Prayer: Gracious God, help us to experience your unconditional love. May we live in such a manner that our minds and hearts might be open to receiving your grace. Grant all people the blessed assurance of your mercy and grace. Then, that peace beyond all understanding will be ours.

Lent: A Serious Season

Readings: Gen 9:8-15; 1 Pet 3:18-22; Mark 1:12-15

Scripture:
"This is the time of fulfillment. The kingdom of God is at hand. Repent, and believe in the gospel." (Mark 1:15)

Reflection: Lent is a serious season since it involves reformation, transformation, and ongoing formation. More, the time is now and Jesus expresses an urgency that we allow God's rule to govern our minds and hearts. Lent is a serious season because we are called to deepen our faith in the good news of God's love and mercy revealed in Christ.

What are the areas, as individuals and as a society, that need reformation? On the personal level, we need but list the capital sins—pride, anger, greed, lust, sloth, envy, gluttony—and we have enough material for reformation for the rest of our lives, not just this Lent. Given our human nature, everyone has to deal with these basic forces that cause chaos in our relationship with God, others, and ourselves. The capital sins are serious matters. In fact, they are matters of life or death.

For God's reign to come, we need the gift of the Holy Spirit, the gift of God's love and mercy. When Jesus went out into the desert and was tested, the Spirit accompanied him. When we are tested in whatever way, we have a resource within us to counter those temptations and remain faithful as Jesus did. Be assured, the temptations will come if they are not already here. Be even more assured that God's Spirit is with us every step of the way, so we need not fear.

There is a "nowness" in our spiritual life. The time of fulfillment is now; God's rule is at hand now! Our task is one of faith: to believe in the Good News. That faith will be tested because our Christian understanding of life is a cognitive minority. Where once Christianity was dominant and the major influence in the Western world, such is not the case in this twenty-first century. What this means is that we must nurture our faith as much as possible through the prayerful pondering of Scriptures, the celebration of the sacraments, and dedicated service to others.

Lent is a serious time and a serious business. We are dealing with our very destiny and must make choices. Do we allow God's kingdom to govern our days or not? Come Easter Sunday, we should have a pretty good read on this question.

Questions: Why is Lent a serious season? What is the one area in your life that cries out for reformation? To what extent does God's will govern your mind and heart?

Prayer: Lord Jesus, once again send the Spirit into our lives. We yearn to do your will but so many forces crowd out your voice and blind us to your presence. Make this season of Lent the greatest time in our lives—a time of growth and renewal, a time of faith and love, a time of praise and thanksgiving.

First Sunday of Lent—C

Lead Us Not into Temptation

Reading: Deut 26:4-10; Rom 10:8-13; Luke 4:1-13

Scripture:
Filled with the holy Spirit, Jesus returned from the Jordan and was led by the Spirit into the desert for forty days, to be tempted by the devil. (Luke 4:1-2a)

Reflection: Temptations come in many forms, but the ancient and universal ones are pleasure, power, and prestige. In the desert,

11

Jesus confronted these idols but remained obedient to the Father. Our Lord refused to use magic to turn stones into bread; he refused to genuflect to the kingdoms of this world; he refused to exercise presumption. And then we read that chilling line: "When the devil had finished every temptation, he departed from him for a time" (Luke 4:13).

Undoubtedly, all of us wrestle with the idols of pleasure, power, and prestige. But there are other temptations as well. One of these is futility, a sense that nothing matters. In a biography of Leonard Woolf, the husband of Virginia Woolf, we are told that while Leonard Woolf was very prolific in writing books, advocating for justice, and traveling all over the world, he ultimately concluded that "nothing mattered." Although that temptation did not paralyze Woolf from acting, it did engender a pessimism that took away his joy of living.

A second temptation that many of us deal with is taking shortcuts. Discipline is not a high priority in our culture. We like to attain things without putting in all the necessary time and energy. How can we achieve our goals with the least amount of work? Ultimately, shortcuts just don't work. There is no other path to the resurrection than embracing our Cross.

And then there is that time temptation known as procrastination. We are tempted to delay that asking for forgiveness, that visitation to a dying person, that card of congratulations. As one saint exclaimed: "Tomorrow may be too late!"

Jesus experienced our human condition from the inside. He knew every temptation but did not sin. We ask for the grace of obedience and fidelity that Jesus exercised.

Questions: What are your personal temptations? What is your understanding of the phrase in the "Our Father": "Lead us not into temptation"? Do you have to wrestle with a sense of futility, taking shortcuts, or procrastination?

Prayer: Lord Jesus, your trial in the desert witnesses to us the full reality of the Incarnation. You took on our human condition in its fullness. You understand our personal struggles from the inside. Send forth your Spirit that we might be obedient and faithful to your Father's will.

Monday of the First Week of Lent

The Right or the Left?

Readings: Lev 19:1-2, 11-18; Matt 25:31-46

Scripture:
"And he will separate them one from another, as a shepherd separates the sheep from the goats." (Matt 25:32b)

Reflection: Courtroom judges have an awesome responsibility as they seek to do the work of justice. They have to separate fact from fiction, make decisions that respect the rights of all, and, in the end, impose sentences that change lives forever. They have the law to guide them, but they have the duty of interpretation and fair application.

The judgment scene in today's gospel seems rather clear cut. Separation of the good and bad is determined by how we treat our neighbor. If we respond with justice and mercy, we are on the right side with the good sheep. If, on the contrary, we have neglected those in need we wind up on the left with those foul-smelling goats. It doesn't take a degree in rocket science to figure out the principle of separation.

But each of us approaches the Final Judgment with considerable trepidation. We come half-sheep, half-goat. On our better days we have reached out to the hungry and thirsty, the stranger and the imprisoned. Yet, we know of times, if not seasons of our life, when we did not clothe the naked or provide shelter for the homeless. We stand in need of God's mercy just as we rejoice in God's affirming of the good we do.

So, the role of the shepherd separating sheep and goats is not as easy as it appears. For this judge, Jesus the Good Shepherd, takes into consideration not only the deed done but also the motive for the action and the circumstances of each person. We may be surprised that many people will be entering the kingdom who, on first glance, did not seem to pass the test that seems so obvious in the gospel.

Here is one of the beauties of the writings of the southern Catholic author Flannery O'Connor. In her short story "Revelation," O'Connor writes about the self-righteous Mrs. Turpin's very disturbing vision. Vast hordes of souls—white trash, freaks, lunatics—were rumbling toward heaven while people like her, noted for their good order and common sense and respectable behavior, were in the rear. How could this be, Mrs. Turpin puzzled.

In the end we do not know the wisdom of God's judgments. What we do know is that God is merciful and kind and that we are to emulate our Creator. What we do unto others, we do unto the Lord. In that message there is no ambiguity.

Questions: In reading the gospel, do you identify with the sheep or the goats or, perhaps, both? Why is it dangerous to judge the behavior of others? When you think of the various images of God, what role does the image of "judge" play?

Prayer: Lord Jesus, help us to understand the deep implications of your parables. You want us to understand clearly that our treatment of others deeply affects you. Give us the courage and generosity to reach out to all those in need. Help us to see you in everyone we meet. May our respect be universal and our compassion inclusive.

Tuesday of the First Week of Lent

Teach Us How to Pray

Readings: Isa 55:10-11; Matt 6:7-15

Scripture:
"In praying, do not babble like the pagans, who think that they will be heard because of their many words. Do not be like them. Your Father knows what you need before you ask him." (Matt 6:7-8)

Reflection: The secrets of prayer are many. But one of them is clear from today's gospel: Many words are not necessary. Babbling gets us nowhere. Rather, the invitation to prayer is to enter into God's presence (more accurately, recognize that we are already in God's presence) and remain as still and quiet as possible.

In teaching us to pray, Jesus shares his own inner discourse with the Father. In his prayer Jesus focuses on the holiness of God's name, the furthering of the kingdom, the doing of God's will. More, we are to ask God for our daily nourishment, commit ourselves to forgiveness, ask to be free of temptation and evil. Nothing is left out. In just a few words we acknowledge our faith, express our hope, and manifest our love for God and one another.

Perhaps the greatest obstacle to prayer is our misconception of God. To think that God needs or is impressed with many words is a failure in our understanding of the mystery of God. Before we pray, God is already seeking us. Before we express our needs, God is already addressing them in his own good timing. Before we attempt to lift up our minds and hearts to the Lord, God is showering us with his love and mercy.

Why pray then? Because when we turn to God in prayer and worship we open our minds and hearts to the graces that already surround us. Not to pray often means that we do not experience God's loving presence. Not to pray is a failure to acknowledge the source of all life and holiness.

In her classic work *Creative Prayer,* Brigid E. Herman writes: "Prayer in its essence is communion with God. The simplest analogy—that of loving, trustful discourse between friend and friend—is also the most profound." One can sense the deep intimacy between Jesus and the Father as we reflect upon the Lord's great prayer.

Questions: What is your concept of God? During this season of Lent, start a prayer folio and place in it your favorite Scripture passages and favorite prayers. What do you understand by the phrases: "Your kingdom come, your will be done"?

Prayer: Lord Jesus, teach us time and time again to pray. So easily we become distracted and verbose. Grant us the grace of silence; grant us the grace of your presence. And when we pray the "Our Father" may we simply listen in on your speaking it to the Father. Through you our prayer takes on a whole new meaning.

Wednesday of the First Week of Lent

Profitable Preaching

Readings: Jonah 3:1-10; Luke 11:29-32

Scripture:
"At the judgment the men of Nineveh will arise with this generation and condemn it, because at the preaching of Jonah they repented, and there is someone greater than Jonah here." (Luke 11:32)

Reflection: In his biography of John Henry Newman, Ian Ker comments that Cardinal Newman "was rather dubious about the value of sermons in general, feeling that 'real profit' is 'the exception rather than the rule.'" Perhaps the great cardinal had a bad day because both Jonah and Jesus were convinced that preaching had some real profit.

For Jonah, not only the townspeople but even the king responded to his warning that in forty days the large city of Nineveh (it took three days to traverse) would be destroyed. A fast was proclaimed, the people turned from sin, and God relented. A considerable "profit" for the citizens of Nineveh.

And Jesus too preached up and down the cities and towns of Galilee. His call was also to repentance and many turned from sin to the grace of the Father. Others, of course, refused to listen and remained in darkness. But the "profit" was considerable and the preaching of Jesus continues today as we ponder the gospel and reflect upon his life.

In another section of his biography on Cardinal Newman, Ker quotes Newman's philosophy of preaching from a different angle of aperture. Newman writes: "Those who make comfort the great subject of their preaching seem to mistake the end of their ministry. *Holiness* is the great end. There must be a struggle and a trial here. Comfort is a cordial, but no one drinks cordials from morning to night."

Jonah was a great preacher calling people to holiness; Jesus was an even greater preacher who not only called people to holiness but showed us, through his suffering and death, how preaching is to be lived out.

Questions: How effective are sermons and homilies in your life? Do they comfort or call you to holiness? Do you ever thank preachers for calling you to repentance and to holiness?

Prayer: Lord Jesus, may your words and the witness of your life continue to call us to a new way of life. Open our minds and hearts to your message of mercy and love. Help all of us to "preach" your gospel by the lives we live. Send forth your Spirit that we might truly be obedient to your word. Bless all those preachers who have helped us to grow in faith, in hope, and in love. We are indebted to them.

Thursday of the First Week of Lent ▬▬▬▬

Asking, Seeking, Knocking

Readings: Esth C:12, 14-16, 23-25; Matt 7:7-12

Scripture:
"Ask and it will be given to you; seek and you will find; knock and the door will be opened to you." (Matt 7:7)

Reflection: Queen Esther, in our first reading, asked that she and her people be saved from their enemies, that their mournings and sorrows be turned into gladness and wholeness. Here is a prayer of deep faith. The Queen believed and trusted in the God of Abraham, Isaac, and Jacob. Dealing with mortal anguish, Esther asked for God's assistance and we know that it was granted.

Besides asking for God's help, we are all searchers. Our infinite longings bump up against our restraining limitations. But it is important for us to note that before we claim priority in our search for God, God is already seeking us out. Like Francis Thompson's "Hound from Heaven," God is pursuing us "down the nights and down the days." Spiritual wisdom tells us to stop and be still. Our frenetic searching must give way to patient waiting. In God's good time we will be found, and in being found, our seeking comes to an end.

Knocking is the third command in today's gospel. Again, the book of Revelation—"Behold, I am standing at the door and knock. If anyone hears my voice and opens the door, [then] I will enter his house and dine with him" (3:20)—reminds us that God is knocking at the door of our heart long before we approach the divine mansion of grace. The question is whether or not we will allow the divine guest into our home.

Abraham Heschel, the great Jewish rabbi, comments: "The issue of prayer is not prayer; the issue of prayer is God. One cannot pray unless he has faith in his own ability to accost the infinite, merciful, eternal God." We all have the capacity to "accost" our loving God, and it is our faith that assures that God will respond by granting us what is best for us and for those with whom we live.

Questions: What are you seeking? In what ways is God seeking you and what are the experiences in which God has found you? Are you hospitable to God's knocking on the door of your heart?

Prayer: Loving God, deepen our gift of faith. You have not only created us to be your beloved daughters and sons, you continue to sustain us on the journey. Our needs are so many; our desires, so great. Please grant what we ask for; please help us to search for those values that are truly part of your kingdom; please open the door of your kingdom to us and all those whom we love. We ask this in Jesus' name.

Friday of the First Week of Lent

Reconciliation: God's Plan

Readings: Ezek 18:21-28; Matt 5:20-26

Scripture:
"Therefore, if you bring your gift to the altar, and there recall that your brother has anything against you, leave your gift there at the altar, go first and be reconciled with your brother, and then come and offer your gift." (Matt 5:23-24)

Reflection: The intimate connection between our relationship with God and our relationship with our sisters and brothers must not be neglected nor underestimated. Love of God and love of neighbor are intertwined. So too if there is disharmony at the human level it is going to impact on our relationship with God.

19

Jesus' vision is one of unity and peace. He came to restore both our relationship with God and with one another. It's all about reconciliation. It's all about dealing with sin in a direct and realistic way. If we have something against another or they against us, the issue must not be swept under the rug.

One might ask how realistic this is since "it takes two to dance." What if one's brother or sister is not willing to be reconciled? Should we then refrain from going to the altar and receiving the Eucharist? As long as we make a serious effort and are persistently open to the healing of broken relationships, we are doing all we can. It would seem, then, that going to the altar and asking for God's assistance and grace would be most appropriate.

In his challenging work *Wounds Not Healed by Time*, Solomon Schimel writes: "It is my belief that the best balm for the resentment, rage, guilt, and shame engendered by human evil is the proper balance of justice, repentance, and forgiveness." It is at the altar that God graces us with justice, repentance, and forgiveness that we might further the kingdom of unity and peace.

Questions: What do you see as the connection between worship and daily life? Is reconciliation possible in all circumstances? Name the people in your life that you have had to go to before worshiping.

Prayer: God of peace and justice, help us to be reconciled with you and one another. We have sinned; we have been hurt by others. We need the gift of your Spirit to bring about the unity that is your will. Guide us in your way.

The Impossible Commandment?

Readings: Deut 26:16-19; Matt 5:43-48

Scripture:
"For if you love those who love you, what recompense will you have? Do not the tax collectors do the same? And if you greet your brothers only what is unusual about that?" (Matt 5:46-47a)

Reflection: Jesus' command to love our enemies seems impossible. We find it difficult even to love our coworkers. We find it difficult at times to love even members of our own family who display irritating characteristics. Yet, Jesus is clear. He even goes on to say that we are to strive for the perfection that God himself has.

What are we to make of this? We must turn to the cross and stand beneath it as Jesus forgives those who are putting him to death. Here we witness a love that would end, once and for all, the death penalty, revenge of any kind, hatred and discrimination. For on Calvary we see the very love and mercy of God manifest. It is nothing short of a miracle.

In our own days we have the witness of Nelson Mandela. Imprisoned for over twenty-five years, this man left his cell and refused bitterness. Though imprisoned unjustly and being the object of ridicule and scorn, Mandela forgave his perpetrators. His example demonstrates the power of grace and gives evidence that "perfection" can be attained.

The old distinction of love the sinner but not the sin has considerable weight. Jesus does not ask us to love what the enemy is doing—be it lying about us, stealing our property, ruining our name. Rather, we are to love the image of God that still resides in the person offending us. Again, without the gift of the Holy Spirit, this is almost impossible.

And as for perfection? Is it not "merely" striving to be the most loving person we can be? On this human journey we will never be without flaws or sins. Yet, there is that call to perfection of never giving up and relying on God's grace that leads to peace, indeed, to a modicum of joy.

Questions: How do you relate to your friends and your enemies? Does anyone consider you an enemy? Someone you have hurt along the way? Are there others besides Nelson Mandela who witness to you the noble task of loving your enemy?

Prayer: Lord Jesus, help us to see into your heart as you ask the Father to forgive those who are killing you. Give us the grace of the Holy Spirit to seek perfection in all that we do so that the Father's will might be accomplished. Too easily we are offended; too easily we hold grudges. Come to our aid. Help us to love everyone and thereby fulfill your command.

Do Not Be Afraid!

Readings: Gen 12:1-4a; 2 Tim 1:8b-10; Matt 17:1-9

Scripture:
But Jesus came and touched them, saying, "Rise, and do not be afraid." And when the disciples raised their eyes, they saw no one else but Jesus alone. (Matt 17:7-8)

Reflection: The sources of fear are many: the unknown, an imminent threat, the possibility of rejection, and the list goes on. Throughout the Scriptures there is a constant refrain: "Do not be afraid." It was this refrain that Pope John Paul II consistently uttered to the youth of the church and the world. The Pope knew how paralyzing fear can be and that it prevents many from living life to the full.

If we were with Peter, James, and John on that high mountain and participated in the experience of the epiphany of Moses and Elijah and then heard the very voice of God, we too would have trembled and been afraid. To still that fear we would have needed Jesus' reassuring touch and reassuring voice. And in the end perhaps we would have been blessed to overcome all fear because we saw the face of Jesus.

And what about Abram? The Lord invited him to leave his father's house and land and venture into the unknown. Surely fear must have crisscrossed his heart. Even though God promised Abram his blessing and presence, still the departure involved some trepidation. Abram's faith was strong, his trust deep. So, even though beyond retirement age, Abram set out as God commanded and we know the rest of the story.

Of all the characters in Scripture, one of the most fearless is St. Paul. He seemed to have found joy and happiness as the hardships and sufferings increased. He was afraid of no one, neither civic nor religious leaders, neither other apostles nor his persecutors. Paul deserved the title "Captain Courageous." His bravery was grounded in the presence of Christ within his life. It was as if he saw no one but Jesus, and in that vision St. Paul found great strength and consolation.

It was the prophet Isaiah who spoke for the Lord in these words:

> But now, thus say the LORD,
>> who created you, O Jacob, and formed you, O Israel:
> Fear not, for I have redeemed you;
>> I have called you by name: you are mine. (Isa 43:1)

Those words should be etched on our hearts this Transfiguration Sunday.

Questions: What are your greatest fears? What does the passage from Isaiah 43:1 say to you? Who are the people in your life who reflect Christian courage and fortitude?

Prayer: Lord Jesus, dispel the fears of our lives. May we trust in your loving presence and live always before your face. We stand in need of courage as we face the mysteries of suffering and death; we stand in need of fortitude as we face life's unknowns and the anxieties of our times. Come, Lord Jesus, come.

The Mountain Experience

Readings: Gen 22:1-2, 9a, 10-13, 15-18; Rom 8:31b-34; Mark 9:2-10

Scripture:
As they were coming down from the mountain, he [Jesus] charged them not to relate what they had seen to anyone, except when the Son of Man had risen from the dead. (Mark 9:9)

Reflection: Mountains stand out not only geographically but also spiritually on our human journey. It is often on the mountain top, in that unique solitude, achieved only through arduous discipline, that we encounter the divine mystery. This was true of Abraham and his son Isaac as they traveled to a height in the land of Moriah. It was on that height that Abraham witnessed his faith and received from God the promise of many descendants.

Saint Paul journeyed far and wide and ascended the spiritual mountain of God's love and mercy revealed in Jesus. From that height St. Paul returned and encouraged all of us, through his letters and his life, to follow the path of Jesus. This Jesus sits at God's right hand and intercedes for us now. Because God did not spare his own Son, St. Paul became a believer and dedicated his life to winning souls for God. Indeed, who can be against us when God is for and with us?

Peter, James, and John climbed the mountain with the Lord and experienced Jesus in a unique way. They were given a glimpse of Jesus' glory; they were given an insight into how Jesus fulfilled the Law and the Prophets symbolized by Moses and Elijah. Never again would their lives be the same. Like Abraham and St. Paul, these chosen apostles—Peter, James, and John—became instruments of God's plan of salvation.

The great Anglican spiritual writer Evelyn Underhill maintained that "the greatest missionary instrument" we can have is *joy*! What joy must have permeated the mind and heart of Abraham in receiving God's promise and the safe return of his son Isaac. What joy St. Paul radiates as he tells us about God's love revealed in Jesus. What joy Peter, James, and John knew as they ventured down the mountain having experienced the glorious transfiguration of Jesus.

Each of us is invited up God's holy mountain through prayer, sacraments, and service. Each of us, through our baptism and confirmation, is called to share what God gives us in those spiritual heights. Indeed, the Spirit of joy is the grace we are to share in our missionary endeavors.

Questions: How does God invite you into spiritual heights? How has your knowledge of Jesus grown over the years? Do you agree that joy is the "greatest missionary instrument?"

Prayer: Lord Jesus, may we join you in all your travels, be they through the desert of temptations or the heights of transfiguration. Give us the discipline to spend time with you in solitude and prayer; give us the grace to share your love with others and to do that with joy. We long to see your face; we yearn to know your love ever more deeply.

Second Sunday of Lent—C

Friendship, Faith, Holiness

Readings: Gen 15:5-12, 17-18; Phil 3:17–4:1; Luke 9:28b-36

Scripture:
[Jesus] took Peter, John, and James and went up the mountain to pray. (Luke 9:28b)

Reflection: Our Lenten journey is long and arduous. All of us need on our pilgrim way mentors and models, teachers, and witnesses, indeed, heroes. That is, we need companionship that will support us in our joys and sorrows; and, we need to offer that support to others. Jesus taught Peter, James, and John how to pray and how to live. And from those disciples, Jesus knew the gift of friendship, witnessed their faith, and felt the stirring of holiness.

John Henry Cardinal Newman, the nineteenth-century English Catholic leader and writer, spoke about friendship, faith, and holiness, themes that run throughout the season of Lent and are found in a special way in today's readings. Newman wrote: "I wonder how long I should last without any friends about me." When Jesus went up the mountain to pray he did not go alone. In that mountaintop experience, as in the Garden of Gethsemane, his disciples were there, yes, asleep at times, but there. A piece of good Lenten advice: Never travel alone.

Regarding faith, Newman claimed that this virtue "has a depth, a breath, and a thickness; it has an inward life which is something over and above itself; it has a heart and blood, and pulses, and nerves, though not upon the surface." Such was the faith of Abraham. It has its thickness that led to righteousness. Abraham believed in the promises of God and thus entered into a covenant, a deep friendship, that would change human history.

Our Lenten journey is a call to holiness. Again, Newman in his realism gives us some sound advice: "I have ever made consistency the mark of the Saint . . . to do well the ordinary duties of the day." This careful observance of "routine duties," be that doing the laundry, cooking a meal, taking someone to the hospital, plowing a field, is the realm in which we are asked to respond to what God is asking of us in the here and now.

Friendship! Faith! Holiness! These Lenten themes invite us to deepen our discipleship in the Lord Jesus.

Questions: What value do you assign to friendships? How has your faith grown during these first few days of Lent? What duties has the Lord assigned to you? Are you doing them well and with love?

Prayer: Lord Jesus, may we journey up the mountain with you and experience the voice of the Father. We are so in need of your friendship; so in need of a deeper faith; so in need of a fuller response to the call to holiness. Only through the gift of the Holy Spirit will we be able to journey well through this Lenten season. Come, Holy Spirit, come.

Monday of the Second Week of Lent

The Measuring Cup

Readings: Dan 9:4b-10; Luke 6:36-38

Scripture:
"For the measure with which you measure will in return be measured out to you." (Luke 6:38b)

Reflection: I watched the famous cook prepare a meal. Near at hand were measuring cups that remained untouched. Whether it was experience that made their use unnecessary or sheer generosity, an ample amount of ingredients were thrown into the dinner's mix.

God is such a cook. There is no divine measuring cup for divine compassion or forgiveness, only overflowing generosity. That is why we are called to be as merciful and as compassionate as God. The gift given must be given away. The parable of the man who was forgiven a huge debt and then went out to demand repayment of a much lesser amount is sketched forever on the Christian imagination. Lack of compassion and forgiveness means that we have closed ourselves off to those graces of God.

An objection might be raised. If everyone began to be so forgiving would not some individuals begin to exploit such kindness and continue in their unjust ways? That is the chance that God is willing to take. Therefore, we should do the same. To measure is to judge. Perhaps the reason why Jesus warns us not to judge is that human judgment is so erroneous. Caryll Houselander wrote: "Our judgments are always, or nearly always, formed by our own needs and fears and limitations, not by an objective contemplation." Or as a Doctor of the Church, St. John of the Cross, writes: "Such is the lowliness of our condition in this life, for we think others are like ourselves, and we judge others according to what we ourselves are, since our judgment arises from within us and not outside of us."

Back to the kitchen. God's pantry is permeated by love. Behind God's mercy and forgiveness, behind the command to stop judging and condemning, behind the imperative to give is the great mystery of love made manifest in Jesus. Jesus is the measuring cup that has no bottom, for infinite is the mystery of divine grace.

Dante's *The Divine Comedy* contains these lines: "Who art thou that wouldst pretend to judge / With thy short vision of a single span, / Of things that are a thousand miles away?" Our vision is short for we all are myopic. God's vision knows no limits and reaches not only thousands of miles away but reaches light-years down into the human heart. God knows what evils and what goodness lurk in each heart. No one else can or does. We have, therefore, no basis for judging another.

Questions: What is your history of judging others and yourself? Name the people who have refused to judge you. How many measuring cups do you have in your kitchen?

Prayer: God of compassion and forgiveness, transform our hearts. Root out all judgment; fill us with your mercy. Give us the wisdom to see as you see, to love as you love. Only then will peace reign in our hearts and in our communities. Come, Lord Jesus, come.

Tuesday of the Second Week of Lent ▬▬▬▬

Humble Service

Readings: Isa 1:10, 16-20; Matt 23:1-12

Scripture:
"The greatest among you must be your servant. Whoever exalts himself will be humbled; but whoever humbles himself will be exalted." (Matt 23:11-12)

Reflection: Football stadiums are filled with "great" players—talented, powerful, swift, gifted. It is interesting to watch those players who draw attention to themselves by "hot-dogging" (doing dances after a great play) and those who play the game, make the great play, and get ready for the next one. No big deal. Just doing what one loves.

The first type of player exalts himself. His grandstanding says: "Look at me! How wonderful I am! I am the greatest!" By contrast, the second type of player demonstrates a basic humility. His conduct says: "I am using gifts given to me. I'm part of team working toward a common goal."

The first category of players is similar to the scribes and Pharisees who seek places of honor, impose burdens on others, draw attention to themselves. Jesus is looking for a different type of personality to follow him. These individuals are to be servants, doing works not to be seen but because they help others. Humility, that is, living in the truth, is to characterize their lives.

Isaiah the prophet was a humble servant. He heard the word of God, took it into his heart, and shared it with others. He knew himself to be a sinner like everyone else. He must do what God requires of everyone: be cleansed, put aside misdeed, cease doing evil. In all humility, Isaiah sought to learn what was good, to do the works of justice, and to set things right.

Rowan Williams, Archbishop of Canterbury, reminds us: "Christ coming forth to serve at the heavenly banquet. This is the fullness of humility, the humility of love." Humility is basically another term for truth and love. Truth means we live in reality, recognizing that everything we have and are is a gift from God. We cannot attribute anything to ourselves in its ultimate origin. And humility is love in that it leads to service, being for and with others.

Questions: What is your understanding of humility? How is this virtue related to love and truth? Why is arrogance and pride so devastating to our spiritual growth?

Prayer: Lord Jesus, you came to serve, not to be served. Give us humble hearts that we may truly hear your voice and do your will. May the grace of obedience govern our days and the Spirit of love motivate our every action. Come, Holy Spirit, come.

▬▬ *Wednesday of the Second Week of Lent*

Authority: Servant Leadership

Readings: Jer 18:18-20; Matt 20:17-28

Scripture:
But Jesus summoned them and said, "You know that the rulers of the Gentiles lord it over them, and the great ones make their authority over them felt. But it shall not be so among you." (Matt 20:25-26a)

Reflection: Authority comes in many forms and in many ways. Nineteenth-century English Catholic writer Cardinal John Henry Newman wrote: "Conscience is an authority; the Bible is an authority; such is the Church, such is antiquity, such are the words of the wise; such are hereditary lessons; such are ethical truths; such are historical memories, such are legal saws and state maxims; such are proverbs, such are sentiments, presages, and prepossessions." Jesus was going to hand on authority to the apostles. He was deeply concerned how that authority would be exercised. Already we see, through the mother of the sons of Zebedee, the jockeying for positions of honor. Jesus is absolutely clear: his authority is grounded in service. Servant leadership most adequately reflects Jesus' use of authority.

The prophets had authority in proclaiming the messages of God. Jeremiah is a good example. In speaking the truth and calling the people to conversion, Jeremiah is attacked by the people of Judah and the citizens of Jerusalem. They were unwilling to embrace the truth and thus attempted to destroy the message-giver. Jesus too predicted the same fate for himself. He would be condemned to death and be crucified for doing the work of his Father. Yet, truth wins out in the end. He would be raised on the third day.

Authority does come in many forms. Words are surely one expression, but even more impressive and influential is a life lived by the core values of truth, goodness, and beauty. Jesus did that type of living. The prophets did as well. Their authority continues to our day because credibility comes in the practice of virtue.

C. S. Lewis maintained: "Believing things on authority only means believing because you have been told them by someone you think trustworthy. Ninety-nine percent of the things you believe are believed on authority." Jesus and Jeremiah are reliable authorities and merit our belief.

Questions: Who are the authority figures in your life? Whom do you trust? What forms of authority do you have and are currently exercising?

Prayer: Lord Jesus, you invite us to participate in your authority, an authority grounded in service of those in need. Help us to live the Gospel. Make us trustworthy messengers of your love and mercy. May we emulate you in serving others.

Thursday of the Second Week of Lent

Friendly Persuasion

Readings: Jer 17:5-10; Luke 16:19-31

Scripture:
Then Abraham said, "If they will not listen to Moses and the prophets, neither will they be persuaded if someone should rise from the dead." (Luke 16:31)

Reflection: Sometimes we just don't get it. We don't get what is obvious, such as being confronted by someone in need, and then after being told to assist that person, we simply walk away. If the great prophets were not able to convince the people of their responsibilities, why would they listen to someone who was raised from the dead? This gospel passage is a judgment on all of us. We have all neglected, at one point or another in our lives, to respond to what God asked of us.

Jeremiah the prophet raised one of the most troubling questions in all of history:

More tortuous than all else is the human heart,
beyond remedy; who can understand it? (Jer 17:9)

Amazingly, God in his great love became one of us and took on that tortuous heart so that we are all known now from the inside. Even though the gospel seems quite harsh and unrelenting, Jesus uses parable after parable to help us understand that God is compassionate and kind. We need but turn from our sin and selfishness to experience the extravagance of God's grace.

Despite the fact that the human heart is tortuous and our comprehension of situations is often lacking, we must strive to listen and respond to God's daily call. The aim of prayer during this season of Lent is docility to the stirrings of the Holy Spirit. More, it is obedience to the duties that God has assigned to us through our gifts and the circumstances of our life. The call is to listen and to repent. That message came from Moses and the prophets; that call continues to come through Jesus and our sacramental life.

The verse before the gospel captures today's message: "Blessed are they who have kept the word with a generous heart / and yield a harvest through perseverance." Translating this into practice takes both grace and our cooperation.

Questions: Do you experience your heart as tortuous? In what ways do you keep God's word and put it into practice? What messages of the prophets have shaped your life?

Prayer: Lord Jesus, help us to understand your parables. Guide us in the way of simplicity and obedience so that we might do your will. We have too often failed to hear your voice; we have too often not followed your path. Bring us back to you and the grace of your merciful love.

Friday of the Second Week of Lent

Beatings, Killings, Stonings

Readings: Gen 37:3-4, 12-13a, 17b-28a; Matt 21:33-43, 45-46

Scripture:
"But the tenants seized the servants and one they beat, another they killed, and a third they stoned." (Matt 21:35)

Reflection: Reading history can be dangerous to the soul. The record there of so much brutality can sour us toward life. Why so much beating, killing, and stoning? Why do the innocent suffer? Why so much warfare and so little peace?

Even as we read the word of God we have a candid account of much inhumanity. The Joseph story is an example. Here are brothers who cannot stand to look at the youngest and most favored in the family. So deep is the envy and jealousy that they plot to take Joseph's life. And even though we have the musical *Joseph and the Amazing Technicolor Dreamcoat*, such humor and "fun" cannot cover up the horrendous nature of murderous intent.

Of course this story is a prelude to the Jesus story. Here we have the Son of God, the epiphany of God's love and mercy, attempting to convince the people of his day about God's saving plan. But the chief priests and the Pharisees are threatened by such goodness. Whether it is envy or guilt, jealousy or shame, or fear of losing power, they would do Jesus in. In the end, they have their way, but only temporarily. God will have the last word and that word is Resurrection, a whole new life.

Lent is a good time to reflect upon our own individual lives and that of the community in which we live. Are we involved in any beatings, killings, and stonings? Verbal abuse can creep into our lives. Words are used to beat up on others. Killings result from the taking of innocent human lives. Legalized abortion has becoming a way of life (a way of death) in our culture. And although we don't necessarily throw stones, we can hurt others through a nasty stare or sheer neglect.

The parable that Jesus spoke was indeed intended for the chief priests and Pharisees. But let us never forget, it is also intended for peoples of all ages, including ourselves. We have been given a vineyard and we will have to give an accounting of our gardening. Let us not injure the messengers God sends today to see how we are doing. Accountability is not just at the end of life, it is a daily matter.

Questions: What does this parable say to you regarding the circumstances of your life? Is beating, killing, or stoning a part of your history?

Prayer: Lord Jesus, help us to be accountable. You have given us so much and you want us to produce a rich harvest. When your messengers come, may we treat them with respect and receive their evaluation with humility. May we tend your garden well.

Saturday of the Second Week of Lent ▬▬▬

Lost and Found

Readings: Mic 7:14-15, 18-20; Luke 15:1-3, 11-32

Scripture:
But now we must celebrate and rejoice, because your brother was dead and has come to life again; he was lost and has been found. (Luke 15:32)

Reflection: The "lost and found" theme pervades our human journey. That is one reason why St. Anthony is so terribly busy. Be it a ring, the car keys, contact lenses, a sock, or whatever, we are constantly hunting down things that have a tendency (on their own) to disappear.

When the "lost" item is stuff, we can usually deal with that. But when a brother or sister, a parent or child, a friend or neighbor is lost, then we have a right to be deeply concerned. The parable of the Prodigal Son is so powerful precisely because it involves such an intimate relationship: parent and child. The story seems to be going well when, after the prodigal begins his journey home, the father races out to greet him. What a happy ending!

But then complications set in. The son who remained home and did his duties is also "lost." Though nearby, he has a hardness of heart that renders forgiveness most difficult. Anger and resentment course through his being, and when the occasion of the father's mercy presents itself, the elder son loses it. The father pleads for reconciliation. More, the father pleads that rejoicing fill his house because of the younger son's return.

Micah the prophet provides us with a stirring image of God, a God who

> will again have compassion on us,
> treading underfoot our guilt[.]
> [Who] will cast into the depths of the sea all our sins.
> (Mic 7:19)

This Old Testament prophet's image of God takes on flesh in the parable of Jesus. The father of the Prodigal Son, the God Jesus reveals, is indeed a God of compassion, a God who treads underfoot our guilt, a God who throws our sins into the abyss of the ocean. How can we not rejoice?

Would that the elder son had come across Johannes Metz's line: "Our relationship with God is decided in our encounter with other men."

Questions: With whom do you identify in the parable of the Prodigal Son? One or all of the characters? How does this parable shape your image of God?

Prayer: Lord Jesus, during these days of Lent help us to face the mystery of sin in our personal lives. More, help us to perceive your compassion and mercy so that we might experience it for ourselves and then share it with others. Come, Lord Jesus, come.

Third Sunday of Lent—A

Living Water

Readings: Exod 17:3-7; Rom 5:1-2, 5-8; John 4:5-42

Scripture:
"If you knew the gift of God and who is saying to you, 'Give me a drink,' you would have asked him and he would have given you living water." (John 4:10)

Reflection: The two deepest hungers and thirsts within the human heart are for knowledge and love. The question arises: where shall we go for true knowledge and life-giving love? The choices are many. Some seek astrology or alcohol; some seek the Greek philosophers or sexual pleasures; some seek science or friendship.

The Samaritan woman at the well came for water. She had made the trip often. Here was the gift that sustained her physical existence. But there was a deeper thirst in her heart as there is in all of us. We thirst for psychological and spiritual satisfaction as much if not more than we do for physical sustenance. When she met Jesus, she came into the presence of God's life-giving water.

Psychologically, Jesus showed her respect. His gaze basically said: "You have great dignity and are loved by my Father. Let me offer you the fullness of life that will lead to peace and joy." We know the rest of the story.

Spiritually, Jesus invited the Samaritan woman into the truth of things. As always, it is the truth that frees us, and Jesus leads her to a self-knowledge that, though humbling, put the cards on the table. She went off to testify to this person, Jesus, who set her free.

One of the contemporary cultural descriptions of the postmodern person is that of a "searcher." In our complex and diverse culture that has so many options, individuals are seeking to find out what is truly worth our time and energy. In a sense, it is putting first things first, having a sense of priority. Another dimension of all this is the hunger for meaning. What is life about anyway? Does it make sense or is our human existence ultimately absurd?

There are many watering holes. Some of them are life-giving and others are toxic. Each of us is invited to approach the well of faith. There, encountering the Lord Jesus, we will come to know God's infinite love and wisdom.

Questions: What watering holes have you gone to over the years? Do you see yourself as a "searcher"? How have you testified to the truth and love you have been given?

Prayer: Lord Jesus, draw us into the mystery of your life-giving wisdom and love. So often we have drunk from the wells of misery and pain. Set us free to find you and grace us with the courage to testify to your redeeming love.

Third Sunday of Lent—B

Good Old Human Nature

Readings: Exod 20:1-17; 1 Cor 1:22-25; John 2:13-25

Scripture:
But Jesus would not trust himself to them because he knew them all, and did not need anyone to testify about human nature. (John 2:24-25)

Reflection: One of the most important and difficult tasks on this human journey is to gain self-knowledge. In one sense, it should be easy since we all share the same "human nature." Apparently, we need but take a few courses in human psychology and we come to a rather clear understanding of who we are. Yet, each of us is so unique, right to our fingerprints and our DNA makeup, that there is no one else like us in the world.

Jesus knew well the bright and dark side of our lives. His respect for every individual, his deep love for family and friends, and his tremendous compassion for all bear witness to a God of mercy and love. But Jesus also knew our dark side. As we read in the book of Exodus, we are given a portrait of humanity that is not complimentary. We are told not to have false gods, not to disrespect God's name, not to violate the Sabbath. More, killing, adultery, stealing and disrespect are forbidden. Here is human nature at its worst.

Saint Paul, in writing to the Corinthians, confronts human nature and its demands for signs and wisdom. Both Jews and Gentiles struggle with stumbling blocks and absurdities on the journey. Paul reminds this faith community that Jesus is the power and wisdom of God. By embracing him and his way of life, we live a truly human life in its fullest sense.

During Lent we are willing to both thank God for making us the way he did as well as realize that there is something radically wrong in life. We call that something sin! Be it turning God's house into a marketplace or coveting the goods of others or being dishonest, we stand in need of God's mercy and love revealed in Jesus.

Questions: What is your attitude toward human nature? How have you grown in self-knowledge during this season of Lent? Do you have someone to talk with about your personal growth?

Prayer: Lord Jesus, you know the human heart, its beauty and its limitations. Send your Spirit into our lives that we might grow in knowledge of you and ourselves. Be our wisdom and our power.

Bearing Fruit

Readings: Exod 3:1-8a, 13-15; 1 Cor 10:1-6, 10-12; Luke 13:1-9

Scripture:
"He [the gardener] said to him [the owner] in reply, 'Sir, leave it for this year also, and I shall cultivate the ground around it and fertilize it; it may bear fruit in the future. If not you can cut it down.'" (Luke 13:8-9)

Reflection: There is an intercession in the Divine Office that might be a mission statement for all Christians: "Lord Jesus, you are the true vine and we are the branches; allow us to remain in you, to bear much fruit, and to give glory to the Father."

We have here the three elements of spirituality: adoration/attention (seeing Jesus who is the vine), communion/adherence (union with Jesus), and cooperation/collaboration (bear much fruit). This way of life applies both to us as individuals and as a community. Attention, adherence, and abandonment to God's will is the Christian way of life.

Jesus' parable is clear: We are to bear fruit. God has gifted us with life and love. Those gifts are to be shared with whomever we meet. The fruits of kindness, gentleness, patience are but a few of the blessings God wants to offer others through us. But bearing fruit is contingent upon our prayer and union with God.

What happened to the fig tree? Surely it was gifted with sun and rain. The soil must have been adequate and the gardener did his duties. But here it was—three years without any fruit. Perhaps the fig tree was greedy and kept to itself all the gifts given. Or, did the tree simply lack gratitude and generosity? Maybe it was just stubborn or wanted to be an apple or pear tree and therefore refused its own identity. Whatever, it was fruitless and faced execution.

Moses and St. Paul were productive; they bore fruit. Moses encountered the living and true God and went on to share God's message with others. Paul encountered the risen Lord and declared Christ as the spiritual rock from whom all life flows. Unlike the fig tree, they lived in union with God through prayer and then responded to God's creative grace by giving life to others.

Questions: What kinds of fruit do you bear in your daily life? How is your ministry connected to prayer?

Prayer: Lord Jesus, you are indeed the Vine. May we remain always in your loving embrace and take the graces given to us and share them generously with others. Do not let us be barren.

Monday of the Third Week of Lent

Speaking of Rivers

Readings: 2 Kgs 5:1-15ab; Luke 4:24-30

Scripture:
"Again, there were many lepers in Israel during the time of Elisha the prophet; yet not one of them was cleansed, but only Naaman the Syrian." (Luke 4:27)

Reflection: Word does get around. A slave girl tells her mistress about a prophet with healing powers and an army commander is cured of leprosy. A king tears his garments and the same prophet, hearing about this, sends word not to worry about who has power over life and death. And even Jesus is the subject of the human "word game." The people in his native village of Nazareth hear about Jesus' prophetic power. They attempt to do him violence because he confronts them about their refusal to accept a messenger from God.

The gospel acclamation contains a lesson concerning words: "I hope in the Lord, I trust in His words; with Him there is kindness and plenteous redemption."

Although ticked off for a while, Naaman, the leprous army commander, trusted and obeyed the words of Elisha and went down to the Jordan river and plunged in seven times. To Naaman's great surprise and joy, the Jordan was a more powerful river than the rivers of Damascus, the Abana, and the Pharpar. Indeed, the God of Elisha was more powerful than all the gods of the Aram. Naaman is converted and turns evangelist: "Now I know that there is no God in all the earth, except in Israel" (2 Kgs 5:15b).

And what about the poor villagers of Nazareth? Not only did they refuse to accept the truth of Jesus, *the* prophet, but they allowed their anger and indignation to carry them to the edge of murder. But Jesus' work was not yet complete and he left his village to minister to others.

Langston Hughes (1902–67) wrote a poem entitled "The Negro Speaks of Rivers." In the verse he tells how he has known rivers and names them: the Euphrates, the Congo, the Nile, and the Mississippi. Though he does not mention the Jordan, Hughes seems to have known the cleansing water of that mighty river as well because his poetry has a prophetic tone. He speaks much truth, truth that was often rejected in his native land of America.

Questions: Who is your favorite prophet? How about Ezekiel (36:24-27) or Isaiah (43) or Micah (6:8)? Do you ever feel like throwing a confronting prophet over the hill (or at least, over your left shoulder)?

Prayer: Lord Jesus, though we often refuse to embrace your prophetic word, do not let us off the hook. Continue to speak to our heart; continue to send prophets into our lives. One day we will listen and be cleansed.

Tuesday of the Third Week of Lent ▬▬▬

A God of Extravagance

Readings: Dan 3:25, 34-43; Matt 18:21-35

Scripture:
Then Peter approaching [Jesus] asked him, "Lord, if my brother sins against me, how often must I forgive him? As many as seven times?" Jesus answered, "I say to you, not seven times but seventy-seven times." (Matt 18:21-22)

Reflection: One of the qualities of God revealed in Jesus is that of "extravagance." As Creator, God multiplied the stars of heaven and the sands on the shores of the seas. As Redeemer, God extends his limitless mercy to all nations. We should be overwhelmed by such extravagance. More, we should come to realize that, made to the image and likeness of this God, we are to emulate that divine extravagance by our own extravagance of love and forgiveness.

But there is something frugal about the soul. There is something awry in our human condition. We tend to pinch pennies and be niggardly in dishing out to others the abundance that God has showered down upon us. Such economy is not to be condoned. Such frugality and tight-fistedness lead us down a dead-end road.

The gospel parable should startle us. All of us have been forgiven so many times by our gracious God. And yet, injured by others, we tend to hold grudges, become passive-aggressive, and shun such people even for a lifetime. Jesus is clear: We must forgive our brothers and sisters from the heart.

Cardinal John Henry Newman, in a letter to E. B. Pusey, wrote: "I would not give much that love which is never extravagant, which always observes the proprieties. . . . What mother, what husband or wife, what youth or maiden in love, says but a thousand foolish things, in a way of endearment, which the speaker would be sorry for strangers to hear; yet they are not on that account unwelcome to the parties to whom they are addressed."

When it comes to forgiveness, God does not observe the proprieties as Peter would attempt to do. Nor should we. We must not forget that the measure we measure out will be measured unto us—so sayeth the Lord.

Questions: How extravagant is your love and your mercy? How many times have your friends and family members forgiven you? Why is frugality at once a blessing and a curse?

Prayer: Lord Jesus, you witness for us the extravagant mercy of the Father. From the cross, you forgave your executioners. From heaven still, you forgive us and call us to forgive one another. Send your Spirit of mercy into our hearts. Grant us your peace.

Wednesday of the Third Week of Lent

The Law, the Prophets, the Christ

Readings: Deut 4:1, 5-9; Matt 5:17-19

Scripture:
[Jesus said to his disciples:] "Do not think that I have come to abolish the law or the prophets. I have come not to abolish but to fulfill." (Matt 5:17)

Reflection: In John's gospel, we are reminded that Jesus came that we might have the fullness of life (John 10:10). Because there are so many paths to life in abundance, we must be open to the various avenues that guide us toward truth, goodness, and beauty. Different cultures and different personalities respond in diverse ways to the grace of God.

Law is a significant highway. Moses articulated God's plan in the great Ten Commandments. This road map has been tested and proven true. Keep the commandments with a willing heart and life will abound. Disobedience here, as Moses so often tells us, leads to death not only spiritually, but in other ways as well. Moses is clear about what brings about life or death, and he begs his people to choose life.

Prophets, those special envoys of God, shouted (sometimes whispered) from the housetops, God's dream that justice and peace would reign among peoples and nations. Their strong and unrelenting voices can still be heard echoing down the centuries. Would that we have ears to hear; would that we have the courage to follow their wise advice. We are indebted to Isaiah and Jeremiah, to Hosea and Ezekiel. They often gave up their own plans to do the work of the Lord.

Then there is Jesus, the full manifestation of the mystery of God, who embodies in his attitudes and behavior the kingdom of God. In Jesus, we witness Truth, Charity, Freedom, and Justice. Indeed, Jesus is the way, the truth, and the light. But he did not downplay the role of His ancestors and tradition. His task was to bring God's plan of universal restoration to its fullness. And the price? The giving of his life!

Question: What is your attitude to law and to the prophets? What is your attitude toward Jesus? How do we in our contemporary culture live life to the full?

Prayer: Lord Jesus, grant us the wisdom to understand the meaning of your commandments and the message of your prophets. Our wisdom is so shallow, our insights so limited. It is only with the help of your grace that we will be able to understand and do your will. Come, Holy Spirit, come.

Thursday of the Third Week of Lent

Demons

Readings: Jer 7:23-28; Luke 11:14-23

Scripture:
"But if it is by the finger of God that [I] drive out demons, then the kingdom of God has come upon you." (Luke 11:20)

Reflection: Sometimes the term "demon" refers to an evil spirit, sometimes to undesirable traits or emotions that we all have to contend with. As the saying goes: "We all have our demons." The question is what effect do they have on our lives and the lives of others? Will they govern our attitudes and behaviors, or will they be driven out of our souls by the grace of God?

Jesus was in constant battle with the demons. He came to bring us freedom so that we might live as the daughters and sons of God. What the demons are about is disunity, a breaking apart of what God wanted to be unified. The demons scatter our energies and cause confusion. The demons blind us to truth and make us mute when we should proclaim the justice of God.

In his day, Jeremiah also contended with demons. One of the strongest was "the hardness of evil heart." It was this hardness, at times meanness, that caused disobedience and the inability to be able to listen to God's word. Thus, the prophet cries out that faithfulness has vanished from the land and human discourse no longer proclaims the message of God.

What are the demons of our time? One is the radical individualism that focuses energy and time just upon oneself or one's family or nation. The self-referential life, based upon a false self-reliance, renders community impossible. Then there is the demon of consumerism wherein we seek happiness in having more and more and more. Such filling-up leaves us empty, indeed, sad. Things cannot bring us the joy and peace that are the byproducts of loving relationships. A third demon is violence and incivility. We have to a large extent lost a reverence for life, a respect that protects and promotes human dignity.

Jesus wants to drive out all demons. Lent is a season for naming those spirits and submitting them to the Lord's healing grace.

Questions: What are your personal demons? Greed? Lust? Pride? Anger? How do they find expression? How can they be driven out of your heart?

Prayer: Gracious and loving God, we struggle with our demons, powerful forces that would separate us from you and one another. Come and drive them out. Free us to listen to your word and to do your will. Only then will we know true happiness and peace.

Friday of the Third Week of Lent

Loving Unreservedly

Readings: Hos 14:2-10; Mark 12:28-34

Scripture: "Hear, O Israel! The Lord our God is Lord alone! You shall love the Lord your God with all your heart, with all your soul, with all your mind, and with all your strength." (Mark 12:29b-30)

Reflection: Love goes in two directions: vertically, to God, and horizontally, to one's neighbor. Love is inclusive and demanding; love is the bottom line of spirituality and religion. And why? Because God is love.

Hosea the prophet knew about this God, loving and merciful and gracious. The prophet uses the image of dew to describe God's affection for his people, dew that moistens and gives growth. Love is life-giving; love is fruitful. Thus, the prophet attacks all those attitudes and behaviors that diminish life and cause great harm; all those anti-love forces that restrict and narrow the soul. Hosea challenges the people to repent and be compassionate as God is compassionate.

Those who love are not far from the kingdom of God. In fact, by being a loving person we are in God's domain and doing God's will. Understanding and prudence, wonderful as they are, are not sufficient. Love demands action, a response that conforms our lives to God's image and likeness. For sinners, this path of compassionate love is a stumbling block since we are enslaved in our selfishness and narcissism.

What is being asked for is not a partial but a total love. With all one's heart, soul, mind, and strength. Perhaps the adverb "unreservedly" captures the commandment of God. We are to love God and our neighbor without reservation, without holding back the tremendous grace that God first showered upon us. This is what Jesus' self-giving is all about. This is the meaning of the paschal mystery of Jesus' life, death, and resurrection. It is a total and absolute commitment to God's kingdom, to God's will.

Questions: To what extent do you love God and those God has sent into your life? Would you characterize it as a love without reservation? Is such loving possible given our human condition?

Prayer: Lord Jesus, may we not only hear but adhere to your commandment of total love. Send your Spirit into our hearts and into our communities so that we might follow your example of total self-giving. With you, all things are possible.

Saturday of the Third Week of Lent

Humility: The Divine Achilles Tendon

Readings: Hos 6:1-6; Luke 18:9-14

Scripture:
". . . for everyone who exalts himself will be humbled, and the one who humbles himself will be exalted." (Luke 18:14b)

Reflection: Back on Ash Wednesday, the Lord instructed all of us to do three things: pray, fast, give alms. Do these things, it would seem, and one is in good graces with God, that is, one is righteous and justified. Yet there is an old principle that must be attended to, namely, do the right thing and do it in the right way.

The Pharisee in the gospel parable did the right thing. He prayed. Part of his prayer was gratitude in that he thanked the Lord for not being dishonest, adulterous, or greedy, like so many other people. He also fasted and did that several times a week. Add to this the fact that he gave alms, tithing his gross income. What a guy! Certainly, he is a candidate for canonization.

But there was something wrong, drastically wrong. The Pharisee had two radical flaws. His inner attitudes discolored all his "good" deeds. On the one hand, he lived with the conviction that he owed his "righteousness" to himself. Wrong! No one is justified by his own merits but through the grace of God working within him. Second, in looking around at his fellow human beings—yes those greedy, dishonest, adulterous wretches—he despised them. This self-exaltation and holding others in contempt was his downfall. He left the Temple area worse than when he came.

Then we have the tax collector. He probably, like the rest of us, struggled with greed, did not always tell the truth, and had to battle with lust and other sexual temptations. Standing before the

Lord in the Temple—indeed, at a good distance—all he could do was plead for mercy. His humility won the forgiveness of God, and the tax collector left the Temple area justified, his relationship of friendship with the Lord once again restored. The insight of Simone Weil is on target: "Humility exerts an irresistible power upon God." God does seem to be vulnerable to this virtue of humility that puts us in the land of truth. The tax collector, not the Pharisee, was graced with self-knowledge and that grace led to freedom.

Questions: How is it that we can do the right thing in the wrong way? Why is humility such a central virtue?

Prayer: Gracious God, have mercy on us all. Make our prayer sincere; make our lives in the pattern of your Son. We have all sinned and stand in need of your forgiveness. Grant us a humble heart that we might hear and do your will.

Fourth Sunday of Lent—A

The Gift of Sight

Readings: 1 Sam 16:1b, 6-7, 10-13a; Eph 5:8-14; John 9:1-41

Scripture:
As he [Jesus] passed by he saw a man blind from birth. (John 9:1)

Reflection: The gifts of sight and hearing must not be taken for granted. Anyone who has seen William Gibson's *The Miracle Worker* (1962 movie) is given entrance into the world of a deaf and blind person, Helen Keller. Helen connects with a larger world through the guidance and love of her teacher, Annie Sullivan. Where there was darkness, now there is light.

Saint Paul knew darkness, the darkness of his own sin and fanaticism. But when Jesus broke into his life, Paul turned from deeds of darkness to the light that produces every kind of goodness. Jesus was the light of the world, its justice and its truth. It is this Christ who brought sight to the blind man in the gospel, to Paul who was persecuting the church, to the Ephesians who once lived in darkness, and to us in the twenty-first century who are struggling to be good, just, and truthful.

The theme of light and darkness is also present in the first reading as a discernment process is under way regarding the selection of a future king. Samuel is the Lord's agent, and it is among the sons of Jesse that the king will be found. But which one? Seven sons are presented but, according to the light and understanding that Samuel has, none of these is to be anointed king. Upon further questioning, it is discovered that the youngest son, away tending the flocks, is the Lord's choice. We are told that humans judge by appearance—stature, good looks, intelligence—but God looks to the heart. It is in this light that David is judged worthy of the office of king.

We read in the book of Genesis: *fiat lux!* Let there be light. Our God, revealed in Jesus, is a God of light and not darkness, of love and not indifference, of life and not death. Our Lenten call is to be agents of that divine light and to scatter the darkness of sin in our own hearts and in the world.

Questions: Who are the people who have been light-bearers to you, who have helped you to see? Into what regions has God called you to go and bring his light? Watch *The Miracle Worker* and pull out the themes of light and darkness.

Prayer: Jesus, you are the light of the world. There are so many dark areas in our minds and hearts, indeed, throughout the world. Help us to see your presence and to hear your word. Guide us in the way of peace.

Fourth Sunday of Lent—B

A God of Love and Mercy

Readings: 2 Chr 36:14-16, 19-23; Eph 2:4-10; John 3:14-21

Scripture:
For God so loved the world that he gave his only Son, so that everyone who believes in him . . . might have eternal life. (John 3:16)

Reflection: Pope Benedict XVI made a clear and definite statement in reminding all of us that God is Love. His first encyclical letter, *Deus Caritas Est*, spells out his faith in this fundamental tenet. Pope John Paul II made a clear and definite statement when, in his encyclical letter *Dives In Misericordia*, he proclaimed that God is rich in mercy. And the most recent Doctor of the Church, St. Thérèse of Lisieux, records in her autobiography that her God is a God of love and mercy.

Of course, the source of these insights is Scripture. It is in John's gospel that we are told how much God loves the world. That love is demonstrated in the gift of the Son. Even more, the coming of the Son is not for condemnation but salvation. Nothing, not even death on the cross, is too much of a price to pay for the redemption of the human family.

Saint Paul experienced the richness of God's mercy in his conversion from darkness to life. Paul is overwhelmed by the wealth of God's favor in Christ and will spend the rest of his life proclaiming the person of Christ through whom we have been given a share in eternal life. Saint Paul is also very clear that whatever good is accomplished is ultimately a gift from God. Pride has no place in the life of a disciple.

God's love and mercy comes to us in many ways: creation, friendships, talents. A special avenue is the sending of prophets who, generation after generation, draw our attention away from superficial things to the heart of the matter. Unfortunately, as recorded in the first reading, the prophets are often dismissed, even despised and scoffed at. Their message is fundamentally one of God's concern for us and a call that we leave the land of darkness for the land of light. Whenever the prophets are disregarded or rejected, tragedy awaits that generation.

One of the greatest obstacles to a healthy spiritual life is a misunderstanding of the nature of God. That is why Pope Benedict XVI, Pope John Paul II, and St. Thérèse have been sent to help us see that God is a God of love and mercy.

Questions: How has your concept of God grown over the years? Why is a distorted image of God so devastating to the spiritual life?

Prayer: God of love and mercy, help us not only to know you but to experience your compassion and tenderness. Continue to reveal yourself to us through the prophets and teachers who enter our lives. Open our minds and hearts to your revelation.

The Ministry of Reconciliation

Readings: Josh 5:9a, 10-12; 2 Cor 5:17-21; Luke 15:1-3, 11-32

Scripture:
"But now we must celebrate and rejoice, because your brother was dead and has come to life again; he was lost and has been found." (Luke 15:32)

Reflection: The Jesuit poet Gerard Manley Hopkins wrote: "piecemeal peace is poor peace." And so, indeed, it is. Yet, on this perilous human journey that involves so many potholes and broken relationships, perhaps even "piecemeal peace" is a tremendous grace.

In the story of the Prodigal Son we witness that partial peace. The younger son returns home. He who was dead and lost is now back home. There is a restoration of a relationship that had been broken by sin. What joy! What a time to celebrate this renewed unity. What peace was offered to this family through forgiveness and reconciliation.

But the elder son could not enter into the festivity. He felt slighted and was deeply hurt. So the poor father, just reconciled with one son, faces a fragmentation with the other. The father's peace is piecemeal when it should have been whole. Such is the human condition.

By way of analogy, our relationship with our Father-God might be imaged as vertical. Our relationships with our sisters and brothers might be seen as horizontal. The point is that these two dimensions are connected. The vertical relationship affects the horizontal and vice versa.

When the prodigal son's father forgave his son and threw him a party, the "vertical" relationship was restored. Yet, there was still bad blood in the heart of the elder son so that the "horizontal" relationship was disturbed. So the father's peace was partial, still in need of completion.

When the risen Lord appeared to the frightened disciples, the gift that he gave them was peace. It was the gift of reconciliation. Indeed, it was the very gift of the Holy Spirit. Reconciliation is about the union and unity that Jesus came to bring: union with God and unity among ourselves. God's plan is peace, the fullness of friendship with God. The cause of that union and unity is love, the two byproducts: peace and joy.

So, even though the peace was piecemeal, there had to be a celebration since a lost son had been found, a dead son brought back to life.

Questions: Why is our peace and joy always piecemeal on this human journey? Can you live with partial peace and joy?

Prayer: Merciful and gracious God, send your love into our hearts so that the unity you desire might be achieved. May your Spirit of peace and joy permeate our world and our communities. Help us to be agents and ambassadors of reconciliation.

Monday of the Fourth Week of Lent

The Grace of Seeing

Readings: Mic 7:7-9; John 9:1-41

Scripture:
Then Jesus said, "I came into this world for judgment, so that those who do not see might see, and those who do see might become blind." (John 9:39)

Reflection: The great Southern Catholic writer Flannery O'Connor reflects on her mission as a writer: "I am interested in making a good case for distortion, as I am coming to believe it is the only way to make people see."

Jesus' mission involved sight, helping people to see reality for what it is. Throughout the gospel we hear about how Jesus confronts blindness, ignorance, and stupidity. Jesus came to help people live in the truth of things. In his love, he heals and restores the blind to good health and sight.

Unfortunately, many who think they know and understand the workings of God are truly blind and ignorant. And their stupidity does not remain with themselves. They venture forth and impose their erroneous convictions on others, causing great harm. Though physically their eyesight is not impaired, it is spiritually. They are unable to see Jesus as the light of the world and the manifestation of God's truth and love.

The American essayist Ralph Waldo Emerson wrote: "As I am, so I see." Our seeing and hearing depend to a large extent on who we are. Our very "being" enables or thwarts our vision. That is why Jesus is always calling everyone to abandon the ways of darkness and to become disciples of light and love. Sight comes with conversion. By putting on the mind and heart of Christ, we begin understanding the meaning of life and what our unique calling is—to love.

But we cannot love someone or something if we don't know, if we don't see. So Jesus came to give us insight into the mystery of life. He offered the grace of vision. Those who were open to it became disciples; those who thought they were in the know walked away blind and lost.

Questions: What "insights" has the Lord granted you on your journey? How do you help other people to see and to love?

Prayer: Lord Jesus, remove the spiritual cataracts that blur our vision of your Father's love and mercy. We need the grace of wisdom and understanding to comprehend your ways. We need the grace of conviction and courage to live. Heal our blindness and grant us your peace.

Tuesday of the Fourth Week of Lent ———

The Healing Ministry

Readings: Ezek 47:1-9, 12; John 5:1-16

Scripture:
Jesus said to [the sick man], "Rise, take up your mat, and walk."
Immediately the man became well, took up his mat, and walked.
(John 5:8-9)

Reflection: Sickness hits us at many levels: physical, psychological, spiritual. We are vulnerable to germs, rejection, and sin. Prancing through life, we are suddenly thrown to the ground by diverse diseases. And in some instances, it is questionable if we will ever arise and walk again.

We turn to doctors and psychologists for help, indeed, for healing. In some cases, they say to us: "Rise, take up your mat, and walk." Trained in chemistry and anatomy, skilled in dissecting feelings and emotions, they apply their art to varying degrees of success. But when it comes to sin, they are powerless. For it is sin that alienates us from God and his creation. Sin leaves us prostrate, paralyzing us in soul and sometimes in body.

Jesus came to reconcile us. That reconciliation involves restoring us to right relationships. It is divine compassion and mercy that gets us moving again. Jesus is the divine physician who reaches out to us with plenteous redemption.

Nor will Jesus be put off by ritual legality. He will heal on the Sabbath and in winter, in the heat of the summer, in the beauty of autumn. Seasons and times have no hold on God's infinite compassion. Good will be done; healing will be offered.

Our healing begins in baptism. Born in the human condition, we stand in need of forgiveness from the get-go. It is through the sacraments that Jesus offers his life and healing; it is through the sacraments that the community stands with us on this perilous journey. We are not alone; we need not carry our mat by ourselves.

The doctor in Shakespeare's *Macbeth* proclaims: "This disease is beyond my practice." There is no disease, however grave, that Jesus does not come to anoint and heal.

Questions: From what diseases have you been healed? In what ways have you been called to heal others?

Prayer: Lord Jesus, we have sinned and stand in need of your grace. Come to us with your mercy and healing touch. May we stand up and journey on doing your work.

Wednesday of the Fourth Week of Lent

The Works of God

Readings: Isa 49:8-15; John 5:17-30

Scripture:
But Jesus answered them [the Jews], "My Father is at work until now, so I am at work." (John 5:17)

Reflection: In his poem "Trinity Sunday" the Anglican priest/poet George Herbert (1593–1633) gives us a clear description of God's works. The first stanza reads:

> Lord, who hast form'd me out of mud,
>> And hast redeem'd me through thy blood,
>> And sanctifi'd me to do good.

Our triune God is forming, redeeming, and sanctifying us right now.

God is our Creator, the giver of life. We are formed out of the dust (indeed, the mud) of earth. Creation is not just some past mystery, going back billions upon billions of years. Creation is happening now. Our minds and hearts are being shaped by God's creative energy now. Because of our freedom, we can choose not to cooperate with this formation. We can deny our muddiness, reject God, and even attribute the gift of life to some mysterious "force." But Jesus came to help us to see that all life, all holiness comes from God. God's work is one of creation, the giving and sustaining of life.

God is our Redeemer, a savior made manifest in Jesus. We pass from death to life because of the Blood of Christ, because of his sacrifice on the cross. The work of Jesus is one of resurrection and fullness of eternal life. Jesus came to restore us to the Father. All who embrace Christ as Lord and Savior, and who follow in his way, are destined for the risen life. John's gospel says that we should not be amazed at this because what Jesus told us will come to be.

Our triune God, besides being Creator and Redeemer, is also the one who sanctifies. This making holy, this process of growing to the full stature of Christ, is primarily the work of the Holy Spirit, the Third Person of the Trinity. Our cooperation is called for. Indeed, we are sanctified to do good and holy things. But this is always done with the Spirit as the primary agent.

Isaiah the prophet portrays God as a tender mother who cannot forget her child. Our God is Father and Mother, Redeemer and Friend, Sanctifier and Advocate—a merciful, gracious, tender God who never leaves us alone. And this God invites us to continue his works in our days: to give life, to heal division, to grow in love and mercy.

Questions: What is your image of God? What the marvelous deeds of God that you have witnessed in your faith journey?

Prayer: Lord Jesus, you are the resurrection and the life. Reveal to us your works; give us the grace to participate more fully in the works of creation, redemption, and sanctification.

Thursday of the Fourth Week of Lent

Moses: The Lawyer

Readings: Exod 32:7-14; John 5:31-47

Scripture:
"For if you had believed Moses, you would have believed me, because he wrote about me. But if you do not believe his writings, how will you believe my words?" (John 5:46-47)

Reflection: If you had to appear in court, Moses would be an excellent advocate. When God was angry with his people for worshiping the molten calf, it was Moses, the lawyer, who pleaded their case and "convinced" God to let his blazing wrath subside. Moses reminded God of how God liberated the people out of Egypt, how God had promised them descendants as numerous as the stars, how God also vowed to give his people a land flowing with milk and honey. After these closing arguments, the Lord relented.

Jesus is the new Moses, the one who came to give life and hope to the people through the forgiveness of sins and the conquering of death. But the people of his day and of our own did not and do not accept his testimony. Jesus' testimony was twofold: words and deeds. If the people were unable to accept his words about eternal life, redemption, and compassion, then perhaps seeing his works would bring about belief. Jesus is clear: "The works that the Father gave me to accomplish, these works that I perform testify on my behalf that the Father has sent me" (John 5:36b).

Perhaps one reason why people hesitated to believe in Jesus' testimony was because of the demands it would make on their lives. Father William Reiser writes: "Faith in Jesus should lead to our doing the same work that Jesus does—the work of God—and that work is to gather men and women into a communion of life and love."

That is why Jesus came: to unite all people to the Father by teaching and empowering them to love and thus have the fullness of life. But this work demands deep conversion of mind and heart; it demands self-giving sacrifice; it demands sufferings. Not surprisingly so many walked about and rejected the testimony of both the words and works of Jesus.

Moses was a good lawyer. Jesus is even better. For in Christ we have more than an advocate. We have a Savior and a Friend. No more could be asked.

Question: What testimony do you seek in order to believe? What works or words of Jesus led you to belief?

Prayer: Gracious Lord, deepen our faith. Just as Moses testified to your graciousness and mercy, may we believe in your miracles and teaching. Take away out doubts and instill in us the peace and joy of faith.

Friday of the Fourth Week of Lent ▬▬▬▬

In Cold Blood

Readings: Wis 2:1a, 12-22; John 7:1-2, 10, 25-30

Scripture:
Jesus moved about within Galilee; but he did not wish to travel in Judea, because the Jews were trying to kill him. (John 7:1)

Reflection: Back in November of 1959, two killers broke into a farmhouse in Kansas and brutally killed four members of a family. They left the farmhouse with between forty and fifty dollars. In 1965, Truman Capote's book *In Cold Blood* described in great detail the killings and how those murders impacted the lives of so many.

Jesus was killed in cold blood. As we move toward Holy Week and the events of Good Friday, we read in the Scriptures how the plot is thickening. The inhabitants of Jerusalem do not know who Jesus truly is. They do not know the spiritual significance of his origin or of his mission. And the leaders are out to arrest and destroy him because he is a threat to their power and position. Though Jesus' hour has not yet arrived, it soon will. And we will witness once again how the God-made-man was crucified in cold blood.

In the book of Wisdom we are given a simple, profound insight:

> These were their thoughts, but they erred;
>   for their wickedness blinded them,
> And they knew not the hidden counsels of God."
>   (Wis 2:21-22a)

There is a direct correlation between sight and morality. A good moral life gives us vision and wisdom; an evil life produces blindness and stupidity. In other words, there is a connection between morality and morale.

We live in a culture of violence. So many people are killed on the battlefields, on our city streets, within our homes and villages. The Body of Christ is still being crucified. Lent is a season that calls us to turn from evil and do good. We are constantly challenged by God's word and grace to turn hatred to love and conflict to peace. Jesus came to bring about the kingdom, a kingdom of peace, truth, charity, and freedom. We are to be agents of these graces.

Wickedness blinds. Goodness gives sight.

Questions: In what ways has sin caused blindness in your life? What can you do today to further the kingdom of God?

Prayer: Jesus, son of Mary, grant us vision. Remove the wickedness from our lives that we might truly see you and the Father. We are so blind to your beauty; we are so ignorant of your abundant grace. Send your Spirit to live in our hearts so that we have reverence for all life.

Saturday of the Fourth Week of Lent —————

More than Eloquence

Readings: Jer 11:18-20; John 7:40-53

Scripture:
So the guards went to the chief priests and Pharisees, who asked them, "Why did you not bring him?" The guards answered, "Never before has anyone spoken like this one." (John 7:45-46)

Reflection: In David Remnick's *Lenin's Tomb : The Last Days of the Soviet Empire* we read: "With each demonstration Vaclav Havel's voice grew more and more hoarse, but his expression of liberty and passion transcended the dead language of the official newspapers and Party pronouncements." We don't know if Jesus ever struggled with hoarseness, but we do know that his message of God's love and forgiveness was eloquent and strong.

It is quite a feat to impress guards and other agents of law enforcement. Hardened by the rough side of humanity, they tend to be insensitive to language and human discourse. But Jesus was special. He spoke not only with authority but with compassion. His expressions of God's reign went directly to the human heart and stirred the deepest longings therein. It was the erudite and learned who remained unimpressed because they felt threatened by truth and were too concerned with the origin of the speaker.

Nicodemus asked for a hearing. He was a truth-seeker and wanted to get at the facts before making any kind of judgment. Later, he would come to Jesus in the dead of night to continue his search for truth. We might conjecture that he has been given a high place in the communion of saints for his honesty.

In his *Confessions*, St. Augustine speaks about what God has taught him: "I had learned from you that nothing should be held true merely because it is eloquently expressed, nor false because its signs sound harsh upon the lips. Again, I learned that a thing is not true because rudely uttered, nor is it false because its utterance is splendid." Jesus spoke the truth. We do not know in what tones, whether eloquent or rude, but we do know that it changed the hearts of many.

Question: What weight do you give to eloquent speech? How do you distinguish between utterances that are true from those that are false?

Prayer: Lord Jesus, speak your word to us. Open our ears to your wisdom and give us the courage of obedience. You speak the truth; you came to set us free. Help us to treasure your words and the message of your kingdom.

Fifth Sunday of Lent—A ▬▬▬▬

Troubled in Spirit

Readings: Ezek 37:12-14; Rom 8:8-11; John 11:1-45

Scripture:
When Jesus saw her [Martha] weeping and the Jews who had come with her weeping, he became perturbed and deeply troubled. (John 11:33)

Reflection: In his excellent biography on St. Augustine (*Augustine of Hippo*), Peter Brown states that for this great Doctor of the Church "delight" is the primary source that moves the will to action. Tremendous weight is given to the emotional dimension of our spiritual life and it seems to be verified in today's gospel.

At the death of his friend Lazarus, Jesus is deeply troubled in spirit and profoundly moved by the deepest emotions. No cold stoicism here. Rather, genuine mourning over the loss of the physical presence of a loved one. Jesus shared deeply in the sorrow of Martha and Mary and was not afraid to witness to this grief.

Saint Paul's letter to the Romans does not irradiate a great deal of emotion. One might find this letter similar to a chapter in some abstract theological dissertation at a university. But in fact, Paul was deeply moved by the Spirit of God who dwelt within him. Paul is passionate in speaking of Jesus and our need to belong to him. In the letter to the Galatians, Paul maintains that it is Christ dwelling in him that holds his life together. Augustine knew Paul's writings well and was deeply moved to emulate this apostle to the Gentiles.

Ezekiel the prophet delivers a message from God that is filled with hope. Death has been conquered through the Spirit of God. God has promised to be with his people forever, and this God is both a promise-maker and a promise-keeper. One can sense the deep emotion in Ezekiel's heart as he bears the good news to his people.

Emotions have their place and must be properly assessed. Jesus experienced from the inside what we humans know: that emotions are a powerful source of our action.

Questions: What role do emotions play in your spiritual life? How do you react to the fact that Jesus was troubled in spirit? What is the basis for your actions?

Prayer: Lord Jesus, you mourned the loss of Lazarus. Help us to experience the full range of human emotions. Do not let us become hard of heart; do not let us fail in compassion. Send your Spirit that we might discern what it is you ask of us.

Fifth Sunday of Lent—B

God's Law

Readings: Jer 31:31-34; Heb 5:7-9; John 12:20-33

Scripture:
I will place my law within them, and write it upon their hearts; I will be their God, and they shall be my people. (Jer 31:33b)

Reflection: Someone once said that the secret of religion was the transformation of desire. When our desires, which are so often consumed with self-interest, become centered upon God and God's concerns, a conversion of great depth happens.

Jeremiah the prophet is probably referring to this when delivering the message from God about the covenant. God himself will write the law of love and mercy upon the hearts of people and they will find neither peace nor joy until they live in accordance with that law. When desires are transformed by that covenant, then we become a new people and God is truly our God.

When Philip was approached by some Greeks with the desire to see Jesus we again hear of a longing and yearning for something more. Jesus instructs the disciples about the true way of living: death to self by being for others. The metaphor is simple and clear: a grain of wheat dying unto itself to bear much fruit. This is at the heart of the paschal mystery: the giving of self for others in utter self-forgetfulness. When our desires become those of Jesus, we are on the road to authentic Christianity.

From the letter to the Hebrews we hear more about the secret of Christianity: obedience to the will of God. Jesus, the source of eternal salvation, practiced obedience through his suffering and death. Here is the grain of wheat in action; here is that self-offering for the sake of life. Jesus establishes the new covenant, not of the blood of animals but of his own blood, that we might participate in the fullness of life. Death does not have the final word. Through obedience, God grants eternal life.

We are dealing here with paradox, the apparent contradiction that death leads to life, that by hating life in this world, we preserve it for life eternal. Such is the mystery of grace; such is the glory of God.

Questions: What are the desires that govern your days? Have any of your desires been transformed by grace? How do you deal with the paradox that life comes from death?

Prayer: Lord Jesus, you were obedient to the Father's will. You desired what he desired; you willed what he willed. In that was your peace. Help us to experience the law written on our heart: the law of love and mercy.

Justice and Mercy

Readings: Isa 43:16-21; Phil 3:8-14; John 8:1-11

Scripture:
But when they continued asking him, he straightened up and said to them, "Let the one among you who is without sin be the first to throw a stone at her." (John 8:7)

Reflection: Skipping stones on water is a playful activity, a great summer pastime. Throwing stones at people is criminal and sinful. Although stones lack the dexterity of boomerangs, eventually the ones that are thrown will return home to shatter our glass houses.

Jesus was presented with that old "either/or" option. "Either" you are for the law and its just condemnation, "or" you are for mercy and no condemnation. "Which will it be?" the scribes and Pharisees challenged. Jesus bent down twice and straightened up twice after doing some writing on the ground. When he looked up the second time, all the elders had vanished. Jesus, by turning their attention away from the woman's adultery to their own sinfulness, extended to the scribes and Pharisees God's mercy. He did not shame them nor condemn them. They knew their guilt and slithered away.

When Jesus looked up the second time he saw a troubled woman who had just escaped death by stoning. To her, he insisted on justice in telling her to sin no more. To her, Jesus extended mercy in saying: "Neither do I condemn you." We see here that necessary distinction between the sin (that justice insists must be named) and the sinner (to whom mercy comes because of weakness).

In our second reading St. Paul, a person who knew both the justice and mercy of God, records how Jesus is the central reality in his life and the life of all disciples. Paul knew God's mercy for past transgressions; he knew too of God's justice. His energy was devoted to what lies ahead and not getting caught on his sinful past. The woman in the gospel too knew that God was doing something new in her life. She too strained for what lies ahead: the life of grace, the life of justice and mercy.

Questions: Why do we keep insisting upon throwing stones at others, be they physical or verbal? How do you resolve the dilemma of justice and mercy in your relationships?

Prayers: Lord Jesus, we have all sinned and stand in need of your mercy. Do not let us be self-righteousness. Rather, may humility govern our lives. We seek your mercy and forgiveness. May we share these gifts with all we meet.

Monday of the Fifth Week of Lent ▬▬▬▬

Knowing Christ Jesus

Readings: Dan 13:1-9, 15-17, 19-30, 33-62; John 8:12-20

Scripture:
So they said to him: "Where is your father?" Jesus answered, "You know neither me nor my Father. If you knew me, you would know my Father also." (John 8:19)

Reflection: Knowledge is a tricky business. To come to the truth we can look to reason and evidence; to come to the truth we can look to faith and put our trust in the word of another. Our tradition honors both paths and insists that they do not exclude one another for truth is one and undivided.

Jesus, the light of the world, came to set us free and did so by sharing the truth with us, the truth that his Father is a creator; the truth that he is our redeemer; the truth that the Spirit inhabits our innermost being. Science textbooks cannot demonstrate these truths through logical argument. We rely on revelation and the workings of God in history.

One of the Doctors of the Church, St. Teresa of Avila, reminds us forcefully: "Well, if we never look at Him or think of what we owe Him, and of the death which He suffered for our sakes, I do not see how we can get to know Him or do good works in His service."

As we approach Holy Week, we have the responsibility of "looking" at him. This act of adoration, this contemplative glance, opens us up to the truth and, if we see well, our hearts will also be open and overflowing with gratitude. We owe the Lord so much: our salvation. It is especially in pondering prayerfully the suffering and death of Christ that we will come to realize the horrendous nature of sin and the extravagance of God's love. The Cross should be the university of the soul. All of our knowledge is there displayed.

But maybe one of the reasons for shunning knowledge of Jesus is to avoid having to serve. Ignorance, it would seem, mitigates responsibility. If we do not know that Jesus suffered and died for us, why should we enter into his service? Some might think that this ignorance is bliss, whereas it is the greatest tragedy of all: to live in darkness and not see the light of world.

Questions: How has your knowledge of Christ grown over the years? Which mystery of Christ has been most helpful in your coming to know the Lord and then to serve him?

Prayer: Lord Jesus, you are the light and love of the world. Banish our darkness and ignorance; fill us with your truth. And once we come to know you, give us the energy and commitment to serve you in our sisters and brothers.

Tuesday of the Fifth Week of Lent ────────

Above Things/Below Things

Readings: Num 21:4-9; John 8:21-30

Scripture:
He said to them, "You belong to what is below, I belong to what is above. You belong to this world, but I do not belong to this world." (John 8:23)

Reflection: There is considerable irony in those post office pictures of the ten most wanted people. It is because of their horrendous crimes that they are wanted. The fact of the matter is that they never "belonged" and thus are now wanted so that they might be once and for all removed from society.

A foundational question that we all have to answer is: "To what or to whom do we belong?" Jesus uses spatial images to indicate his commitment. He belongs to what is "above," that is, to what the Father is asking of him. Jesus belongs to the kingdom, that realm in which God's will reigns. His whole life is committed to love and freedom, to truth and justice. Jesus belongs to the work of salvation.

By contrast, there is another alternative regarding our commitments and attachments. We decide on the "below" things, things that while good in themselves remain means to an end. But far too often these "below" things consume our lives. And what are they? Pleasure, power, possessions, and prestige! Again, these are legitimate values if kept in bounds.

The "above" things of Jesus—love, truth, freedom, justice—are the object of that phrase in the Our Father: "Thy kingdom come." We are all called to be agents of God's truth about the dignity of every person and the reality of sin; we are all called to love, that self-giving service to others; we are all called to justice, protecting and promoting the rights of all; we are all called to freedom, leaving behind the addictions, be they physical, moral, or spiritual.

Quaker Jonathan Dale, in *Beyond the Spirit*, got it right: "Our faith values—truth, equality, simplicity, peace, community—are a judgment on the world and our guides to the world as it must become."

Questions: How would you characterize your struggle with the "above/below" values? To whom or to what do you belong?

Prayer: Gracious God, set our hearts on values that are truly significant. We face so many options on our journey. Our world is complex and hurried. Send your Spirit upon us that we might make good judgments and seek always your kingdom.

Wednesday of the Fifth Week of Lent

Presence! Truth! Freedom!

Readings: Dan 3:14-20, 91-92, 95; John 8:31-42

Scripture:
Jesus then said to those Jews who believed in him, "If you remain in my word, you will truly be my disciples, and you will know the truth, and the truth will set you free." (John 8:31-32)

Reflection: Presence! Truth! Freedom! In some way, these three human experiences are closely connected and thereby involve one another.

Presence! How do we remain in God's presence? The fact of the matter is that we are always in God's presence just as a fish is in the presence of water or a bird in the presence of air. The problem is not presence or absence. The question is whether or not we are aware of God's surrounding and redeeming love. The key to remaining in God's word is living mindfully and obediently. Mindfulness means that we make a conscious effort to be aware that God is here, now. Obedience is to live according to God's commandments, thus putting us in a situation of fidelity.

Truth! In a culture of pluralism, in an atmosphere where truth is put into question, we are challenged to have confidence in both reason and faith as we pursue reality. The basic truths of our faith—the truth of creation, the truth of redemption, the truth of sanctification—are the foundations of authentic knowledge. Ignorance means that we will live in the land of falsity; doubt means that we will become paralyzed and forever confused. Jesus points out to us the truth of his Father's will and the way to the kingdom.

Freedom! Our struggle with addictions and other forms of enslavement is fierce. While thinking that we are free, often we are chained to vices and habits that bind and incapacitate us. Jesus came to set us free so that we might truly accept the responsibility of our humanity. Freedom is a weighty gift but one that is so precious. Freedom is both a gift and a responsibility. Only with God's grace will we truly exercise that freedom that makes us daughters and sons of God.

The bottom line is discipleship. We are disciples if we remain in God's word. That word will reveal the truth, and that truth will set us free. Then, and only then, will we be able to dance in the fires of life.

Questions: What word of God remains in you? What are your favorite scriptural passages, the ones you have memorized?

Prayer: Loving God, draw us more deeply into the awareness of your presence. We yearn for the truth; we hunger for freedom. Send your Spirit into our minds and hearts so that we might come into the land of true knowledge and know the joy of true freedom.

The Jesus Question

Readings: Gen 17:3-9; John 8:51-59

Scripture:
Jesus said to them, "Amen, amen, I say to you, before Abraham came to be, I AM." So they picked up stones to throw at him; but Jesus hid and went out of the temple area. (John 8:58-59)

Reflection: Throughout history, Jesus has caused diverse reactions. For some, he is seen as friend and savior. For those disciples he is worshiped as Son of God and Son of Mary. For others, he is simply a very good, moral man, excelling in love and forgiveness, but merely human and does not merit any special adoration. In today's gospel, Jesus claimed that he existed before Abraham. For them, this was just too much. The people considered this blasphemy. They picked up stones to kill him.

Each of us has a Christology, a basic understanding of who Jesus is. Sometimes this theology or understanding is implicit. At other times individuals make explicit their vision of Jesus both in word and by their lifestyle. In other words, one's image of Christ Jesus makes a profound difference in a person's life and destiny.

The church teaches that Jesus was both God and man, having a human and divine nature in one person. Down through the ages there have been believers in this doctrine and those who rejected this understanding of Jesus. We witness both the acceptance and rejection of Jesus in John's gospel during this fifth week of Lent. Jesus attempts to explain to the leaders and crowds who he is and what he is about. Time and time again there is misunderstanding and outright rejection.

Jesus tells the people that Abraham, their great father, was a man of faith. More, God's love for Abraham was manifest in the covenant he formed with Abraham in promising him many descendants and a new land. Then Jesus informs the crowds that, were Abraham in their presence, he would rejoice to hear how Jesus and the Father are one from all eternity. Abraham would have seen that Jesus was eternal and the full expression of God. Abraham would have had no part of their stones and of their plot to kill Jesus.

Would that the crowds could have heard what a rabbi, Abraham Heschel, from the twentieth century had to say: "We cannot live by a disembodied faith." Jesus, through the Incarnation, has made faith an embodied reality.

Questions: What is your Christology? If someone asked to describe who Jesus is for you, what would you say?

Prayer: Lord Jesus, strengthen our faith. You are the revelation of the Father and light of the nations. May we rejoice in your glory and live by your word. May we come to know that because of your life, death, and resurrection, we shall never die.

Friday of the Fifth Week of Lent —————

Our Life's Work

Readings: Jer 20:10-13; John 10:31-42

Scripture:
The Jews again picked up rocks to stone him [Jesus]. Jesus answered them, "I have shown you many good works from my Father. For which of these are you trying to stone me?" (John 10:31-32)

Reflection: Mother Teresa of Calcutta did many good works, assisting the poorest of the poor. The members of the St. Vincent de Paul Society do many good works, helping people who are in need. Catholic Relief Services (CRS) is an organization that goes throughout the world providing resources and aid to individuals of all races and creeds. At the heart of Christianity is the doing of good works and thereby giving evidence of one's faith.

Jesus did many good works. He was on a mission and was obedient to his Father's will. Many of those works involved giving life to others as we witness in the miracles stories. God the Father is a life-giver. Jesus gave life to those who were physically, psychologically, and spiritually ill. He reminds us that he came not for the healthy but for those who need a divine physician. And, of course, we are all in that category.

Jesus did the work of redemption, bringing oneness where there was division and alienation. Next week we gather below the Cross to witness the climax of that work in the crucifixion. Here, in Jesus' total sacrifice of himself, we see the Father's work brought to completion. Love it is that we see manifest on the hill of Calvary. Love it is that lays down one's life for others.

Jesus did the work of sanctification through the gift of the Holy Spirit. Our risen Lord told the frightened disciples not to be afraid but to be at peace. Then he breathed on them and gave them the Holy Spirit, a Spirit that would make them courageous and strong in continuing his mission and ministry.

In Tennyson's *Ulysses*, we read: "He works his work, I mine." Jesus never said this regarding his work and the work of the Father. What they did, they did together: creating, redeeming, sanctifying. What we celebrate is the trinitarian work, a work that offers us salvation and sanctification. How blessed we are.

Questions: What work have you been assigned in this life? What is your life's work? In what sense is that work simply a continuation of the work of Jesus and his Father?

Prayer: Gracious God, help us to understand the vocation you have assigned to us. You have given us time and talent. You call us to share your life and love with others. May we undertake that work with courage and joy. May our lives truly make a difference.

Saturday of the Fifth Week of Lent ▬▬▬

The Dignity of All

Readings: Ezek 37:21-28; John 11:45-56

Scripture:
But one of them, Caiaphas, who was high priest that year, said to them, "You know nothing, nor do you consider that it is better for you that one man should die instead of the people, so that the whole nation may not perish." (John 11:49-50)

Reflection: Throughout his long term as pope, John Paul II consistently and forcefully promoted the dignity of every single human being. No one should be used as a means to an end. Everyone has value and is to be treated with the utmost respect. Although many individuals and nations refused to abide by this conviction, Pope John Paul II never stopped proclaiming the importance of everyone.

As we prepare to enter Holy Week we witness how this value was disregarded by the chief priests and the Pharisees. Jesus was expendable. Kill him and the Romans would have less cause to take away their nation. Wrong on both accounts. Not only were the leaders of the day violating basic morality, but they were denying the foundations of religious belief.

What was going on in the mind and heart of Jesus during these distressing and turbulent days? We can be assured that he focused on one thing: doing the Father's will. If that meant suffering and death, so be it. Jesus' compassionate heart understood the motives of the leaders of his day. He knew their ignorance, their intrigue, their lust for power and control. And yet he never denied them that dignity that is fundamental to Christianity. There was always hope that the blind might see, the lost might be found, the sinner might become a great saint.

Thus, hope is basic to our celebration of our Lord's paschal mystery. We must bring to all these events—be they betrayal, deception, violence—an awareness that something greater lies behind all this. That "something" is the power and glory of a God who loves us and who will save us. Without that hope, we will despair, become hard of heart, and fail to strive to become what God wants us to be: agents of his love and mercy.

Questions: What is your level of appreciation of your own and others' dignity? How do you respond to those who reject or betray you? Is hope the fundamental virtue you ask for as we enter into Holy Week?

Prayer: Creator God, who have made us in your own image and likeness. You, cherish and delight in your daughters and sons. Help us to become disciples of Jesus. Help us to become loving, caring, respectful human beings. Transform our minds and hearts so that we might live as Jesus did.

Palm Sunday
of the Lord's Passion—A, B, C

The Road of Suffering

Readings: Isa 50:4-7; Phil 2:6-11; Luke 22:14–23:56

Scripture:
"I have eagerly desired to eat this Passover with you before I suffer, for, I tell you, I shall not eat it [again] until there is fulfillment in the kingdom of God." (Luke 22:15-16)

Reflection: In *The Measure of My Days* Florida Scott-Maxwell offers an insight into suffering that is truly profound: "If it is only at the centre of our being that suffering is resolved, is it not there that we are nearest to God? Is it even the road to him, if we knew how to travel it?"

Jesus knew the road to suffering, he who was nearest to the Father. It was a road of physical violence and torture, a road of rejection and betrayal, a road of spiritual abandonment of the deepest order. He knew how to travel that road by means of humility and obedience.

Already in the incarnation, Jesus began that self-emptying process known as *kenosis*. On this Palm Sunday we are invited again to participate in this process of humility. In a self-forgotten act of incredible proportions, Jesus focuses not upon his own pain but on the thief who is promised eternal life. Jesus lived the virtue of humility and the humiliation of being ridiculed in public and portrayed as a sinner. All this done to our incarnate God. Such humility.

And Jesus walked the path of suffering through the virtue of obedience. He said yes to whatever was necessary for the redemption of the world. That yes came only after terrible anguish in the garden where, even there, he lacked the human support that he longed for. It was a double pain: the anguish of crucifixion and the want of prayerful companions.

All of us are invited this week to walk the road of suffering. Let us pray that it can be a journey that leads us nearest to our loving, merciful God. May we receive the two graces of humility and obedience that we might walk the road well, in union with Jesus. Already on this Palm Sunday we have hints of Easter joy and peace.

Questions: How do your approach the problem of suffering? In what ways has the Lord invited you to share in his humility and obedience?

Prayer: Lord Jesus, you embraced our pain and suffering with the utmost love. Assist all those who this day face heavy crosses. Help all of us to stay with you on the road to Calvary so that we share with you the great mystery of Easter. We are weak and cowardly. Give us your strength and courage.

Monday of Holy Week

Table Fellowship

Readings: Isa 42:1-7; John 12:1-11

Scripture:
Mary took a liter of costly perfumed oil made from genuine aromatic nard and anointed the feet of Jesus and dried them with her hair; the house was filled with the fragrance of the oil. (John 12:3)

Reflection: On this Monday of Holy Week we witness love and betrayal. Mary, along with Martha and Lazarus, were dear friends of Jesus. Their relationship was special and filled with tenderness, hospitality, and deep care. Bethany was a town that Jesus might have called a second home. How Jesus must have longed to spend as much time as possible in this loving environment.

But, at table in that loving house was a mortal enemy, Judas. He is identified as a thief, as one having no concern for the poor. He stole from the treasury monies that were given for those in need. Add to this thievery Judas's hypocrisy as he pretends to want to reallocate the funds for the oil in the direction of the poor. Sheer pretense! Probably poor Judas was also jealous of the attention given to Jesus by Mary and Martha. The soul of Judas was not a pretty picture.

How does Jesus deal with this love/hate situation? He tells Judas to leave Mary alone. Although unknown to her, Mary is preparing Jesus for his death. This preparation is taking place at various levels. Psychologically, the anointing with oil and wiping with her hair communicated a tender, holy affection. Scripturally, the anointing confirms that Jesus is indeed king, prophet, and priest. And spiritually, the anointing speaks of consecration as Jesus continues his ministry of giving everything back to the Father.

We do not know the thoughts or reactions of Lazarus to this whole event. Several things come to mind as to what they might have been. How proud Lazarus must have been of his sister Mary who expressed to Jesus such respect and reverence, feelings that Lazarus had for Jesus, the one who saved him. How saddened Lazarus must have been at the rudeness and trickery of Judas who, at the table of friendship, continued his work of betrayal. And, as for Martha, how grateful for her service and a foretaste of the paschal meal.

Questions: Have you ever been at dinner where both love and hatred were in the atmosphere? How did you react to these powerful movements?

Prayer: Lord Jesus, as we journey with you this Holy Week help us to enter more deeply into your mind and heart. Give us an appreciation of your love and compassion, of your dedication and mission. May betrayal and thievery be far from our hearts. May our faith in you grow every moment.

A Troubled Jesus

Readings: Isa 49:1-6; John 13:21-33, 36-38

Scripture:
When he had said this, Jesus was deeply troubled and testified, "Amen, amen, I say to you, one of you will betray me." (John 13:21)

Reflection: Back in 1816, the German poet Goethe wrote a poem in which he maintained that if a person was ignorant of the fact that they have to die so as to rise, that person would always be troubled. More, the earth will be a dark place for such a one because the dying/rising process has not been embraced.

During this Holy Week we are invited into the paschal mystery, into the death and rising of the Lord. Even though, like Jesus, this dying process is distressful, it ends in glory for those who are obedient. One of the foundational metaphors in Jesus' life was the grain of wheat and its task of dying to self that it might yield a rich harvest. Goethe understood this imagery and translated it into his verse.

Jesus was deeply troubled on two fronts. Judas, money-hungry and a deceiver, would betray his Master by a kiss and for a few coins. Peter, friend and leader of the disciples, would betray his Lord out of cowardice.

We should pause over the gospel passage: "And it was night" (John 13:30b). It was night for Jesus; it was night for Judas; it was night for Peter. For Jesus that darkness was lived in union with the Father. Though there was little consolation, Jesus, as always, commended his heart and soul to the Father.

For Judas, that night turned into despair. After the betrayal and receiving the blood money, Judas took his own life. The shame and guilt were overwhelming. He could no longer face others or himself. What anguish tore through his being.

And Peter? Into the night he went and wept bitterly. How the sound of the cock's crow must have haunted Peter for the rest of his life. His original pride was smashed to smithereens. Now, a humble Peter would walk the earth knowing no arrogance but only the mercy of God.

Questions: What has been your experience of being troubled? How have you faced the dark night of the soul?

Prayer: Lord Jesus, your love was so deep for us that you embraced the fullness of our human condition. You were troubled, troubled that your dearest comrades would betray you and lose their integrity. May we experience God's love and mercy so that, in our troubled days, we may never abandon you.

Wednesday of Holy Week

The Tragedy of the Traitor

Readings: Isa 50:4-9a; Matt 26:14-25

Scripture:
When it was evening, he reclined at table with the Twelve. And while they were eating, he said, "Amen, I say to you, one of you will betray me." (Matt 26:20-21)

Reflection: There are two names that are synonymous with the term traitor: Benedict Arnold and Judas. General Arnold, a leader in the Continental Army during the Revolutionary War, betrayed his country in plotting with the British to take over West Point. And, Judas, of course, opted for thirty pieces of silver in the handing over of Jesus.

And the question is why? Why would a general betray his country and why would a friend and companion of Jesus turn traitor?

In the case of Benedict Arnold several factors are known. He was passed over in not being promoted; he did not want an alliance with France; and, he married a Loyalist girl by the name of Peggy Shippen. While not condoning what Arnold did, we might begin to comprehend his motivation.

But Judas is another story, one buried in mystery. Was the betrayal motivated by financial gain? Thirty pieces of silver seems an inadequate sum. Was Judas passed over as the leader of the disciples in Jesus' favoring Peter? Did Judas find Jesus' mode of operation to be too nonpolitical? We do not know. All we are given is that Judas did the deed and he was unable to live with himself ever again.

Jesus' appointed time drew near. The Passover was here and the work of redemption was going to be accomplished. If that involved betrayal, torture, and crucifixion, so be it. Jesus would drink whatever cup was necessary for the salvation of the world. One can only conjecture as to the depth of Jesus' anguish over Judas and his fate. Those sweats of blood in the Garden were probably directly related to Jesus' concern for Judas.

Would that Jesus could have been able to say this line from Willa Cather's *My Antonia*: "These two fellows had been faithful to us through sun and storm, had given us things that cannot be bought in any market in the world." But, sad to say, Judas and Peter were not such fellows.

Questions: What do you think were the motives for the betrayal by Judas? Does Holy Week challenge you to question your fidelity?

Prayer: Lord Jesus, you were faithful to the Father's will and the mission of redemption. We struggle in our fidelity; we are tempted to take the easy route and not follow in the way of the cross. Strengthen us in our commitment to discipleship. May we come to know that you are truly our Redeemer and Friend.

Holy Thursday Evening ─────────

The Towel and the Table

Readings: Exod 12:1-8, 11-14; 1 Cor 11:23-26; John 13:1-15

Scripture:
So when he had washed their feet [and] put his garments back on and reclined at table again, he said to them, "Do you realize what I have done for you?" (John 13:12)

Reflection: There is a common expression that articulates well a universal experience: "He/She just doesn't get it!" In our own lives, we so often just don't get it: get that we are loved and forgiven by God, get that we are gifted beyond measure, get that we stand in need of God's mercy and compassion. In other words, we walk around ignorant of grace and sin, of beauty and possibilities. We just don't get it!

Lest we feel discouraged, the disciples of Jesus had a difficult time understanding what it was that he did for them in the washing of their feet and in the breaking of bread. It was at this table, the table of the Last Supper, that God revealed divine love in concrete terms: a towel and bread, in service and total self-giving. No one could imagine that the Messiah would take on such lowliness and such humility. So Jesus' question—"Do you realize what I have done for you?"—was one that would take years to understand. We, two thousand years later, are still struggling to comprehend the depth of God's love.

The towel and the table! The towel is an instrument of a servant. We should not limit the cleansing of the disciples' feet to just the washing of the flesh. Jesus' towel cleansed their minds, hearts, and souls as well. The gesture of kneeling before another highlights the voluntary poverty that Jesus took upon himself. Trying to realize all this demands the deepest faith.

And the table! Saint Paul's whole life was centered on this event of Jesus giving us himself in the bread and wine. The great apostle to the Gentiles handed on what he had received. His whole ministry was an attempt to help people realize what Jesus had done and was doing in their lives.

In the end, the towel and the table are about liberation. Jesus sets us free from darkness and ignorance. We are given a God of total self-giving and extravagant love.

Questions: What do the towel and table symbolize for you? How have you grown in your understanding of the Eucharist over the years? Do you realize what Jesus is doing for us?

Prayer: Lord Jesus, grant us the gift of wisdom to understand the meaning of the Eucharist in our lives. May we see in the bread that is broken the gift of your life. May we see in the washing of the feet the towel of humility. May we never depart from your table and may we commit ourselves to a life of service.

Good Friday of the Lord's Passion

A Suffering God

Readings; Isa 52:13–53:12; Heb 4:14-16; 5:7-9; John 18:1–19:42

Scripture:
Then Pilate took Jesus and had him scourged. And the soldiers wove a crown out of thorns and placed it on his head, and clothed him in a purple cloak. (John 19:1-2)

Reflection: Suffering happens at so many levels. The body can be tortured with scourging; the mind and heart suffer from rejection and betrayal; the spirit can experience abandonment and terrifying loneliness. Human history records so much pain and agony, so much so that the question of the providence of God is continually raised. If God is good and almighty, how can there be so much suffering in the world?

We are here in the land of mystery. Our finite human minds cannot comprehend nor explain the enigma of suffering. But the Christian does have a response. At the core of Christianity is the paschal mystery, the conviction that through the life, suffering, death, and resurrection of Jesus, we have been given a path to eternal life. This belief does not explain human suffering. Rather, it maintains that our Incarnate God came among us to share in the sorrows and joys of our human journey.

On Good Friday we make our way to Mt. Calvary and embrace the mystery of the Cross. No explanation here; no grand theory of redemption for most of us. Rather, we participate in the mystery by contemplating a sacrificial love that sets us free. Silence is the proper response; adoration, our prayer.

In his work *Christian Hope* the great theologian John Macquarrie comments: "But it was precisely His passion which opened the new and deeper understanding of God as one who stands with His creatures amid the sins and sufferings of the world, and is not therefore a distant celestial monarch, untouched by the travail of creation."

What Good Friday does is to revolutionize our very understanding of God. And thus, as a corollary, it changes our understanding of ourselves. We, who are made in the image and likeness of God, are to become more and more involved in the travails of the world. We now have no excuse to remove ourselves from the joys and sorrows of life. As someone once said: "Go where the suffering is." Jesus did that and we, as his disciples, are to do the same.

Questions: What does Good Friday teach you about the mystery of God? Are you willing to go where the suffering is?

Prayer: Lord Jesus, you gave yourself totally to our human condition. You embraced our joys and our sorrows, and for that we are deeply grateful. Teach us to follow in your way. May we never shun the Cross out of fear. Send your Spirit of courage into our hearts.

Holy Saturday Night: The Easter Vigil

All These Things

Readings: Ezek 36:16-17a, 18-28; Rom 6:3-11; Luke 24:1-12

Scripture: Then they returned from the tomb and announced all these things to the eleven and to all the others. . . . but their story seemed like nonsense and they did not believe them. (Luke 24:9, 11)

Reflection: Some news seems too good to be true. The good news of Jesus' resurrection dumbfounded the disciples and, though amazed, they could not comprehend that the power of death and sin had been conquered through Jesus' suffering, death, and resurrection. The women's report of "all these things" did not make sense. Their story fell on unbelieving ears.

What are "all these things?" First of all, the gift of life! "Why do you seek the living one among the dead?" (Luke 24:5b). Our Creator God is a God of life. The mystery of the resurrection is directly related to the mystery of creation. It's all about life, life to the full. Death does not have the finality that our culture attributes to it. It is a doorway, a portal, a gateway into eternal life for the person of faith.

"All these things" is about redemption. Because of Adam's sin and our own, we have been enslaved by our selfishness and destructive behavior. We all stand in need of a savior, one who showers us with mercy and the gift of eternal life. Jesus is our beautiful Redeemer, the one who laid down his life for our salvation.

And "all these things" is about the gift of the Holy Spirit. Repeatedly, Jesus told the apostles that he must return to the Father if the Spirit is to be given to them. Jesus promised them this Gift, the very gift of the triune life. It would be the power of the Spirit that would give the disciples courage and wisdom, enthusiasm and peace.

This good news has astounded people for centuries. For those who accept it and live it, great joy comes into their hearts. For those who reject or doubt "all these things," much sadness and confusion.

Questions: Whom do you identify with in the gospel passage proclaimed on this Easter Vigil? Have you taken the "good news" to heart? How has that news affected your everyday life?

Prayer: Risen Lord, open our minds and hearts to the good news of your love and mercy. You are indeed our Friend, Redeemer, and Brother. May we continue your mission and ministry of reconciliation and become more dedicated instruments of your peace and joy.

Easter Sunday:
The Resurrection of the Lord

Jesus: Present and Manifest

Readings: Acts 10:34a, 37-43; Col 3:1-4; John 20:1-9

Scripture:
Then the other disciple also went in, the one who had arrived at the tomb first, and he saw and believed. For they did not yet understand the scripture that he had to rise from the dead. (John 20:8-9)

Reflection: In the early church, Easter began with a greeting extended to fellow Christians: "Christ is risen." And the immediate response would be: "Christ has risen indeed and has appeared to Simon."

We might ask on this day of joy how the Lord has appeared to us. Just as the risen Lord became present and manifest to so many in the early days of Christianity, that same Lord comes to us under many disguises. We need the eyes of faith to recognize and then respond to Jesus who still lives among us.

The most obvious appearance is in our sacramental life. At the Easter Vigil, thousands of individuals entered the church through baptism and the conferral of confirmation. Jesus appeared through the words and actions of the church's ritual. And then, most clearly, Jesus is seen in the Eucharist wherein we again hear his words—"This is my body given for you; this is my blood shed for you." In joy we respond by proclaiming the mysteries of our faith.

The risen Lord comes also through the believing community. We see Christ present and manifest in the cry of a newborn infant, in the human concerns committee that serves the poor, in the parents who sacrifice their lives for their children. Jesus lives within us and continues to express his love and compassion in thousands of ways.

The risen Lord appears in a special way in those who suffer. Jesus carried into his new life the wounds on his feet and hands, the scar left where the spear pierced his side. The risen Lord continues to be the Suffering Servant, and we recognize him in all those who participate in his suffering and death.

There are two great Easter gifts: faith and peace. We ask for the gift to believe in the mystery of God's love and mercy; we ask for the grace of peace that will forever be beyond our understanding.

Questions: How do you recognize the risen Lord in today's world? What is your response to his visitations in your life?

Reflections: Risen Lord, deepen our faith. You are truly here among us in so many ways. Remove our blindness and hardness of heart. Open our minds to understand your love and instill in us a reverence for your abiding presence. Come, Lord Jesus, come.

The Keys of the Kingdom

Readings: 1 Pet 5:1-4; Matt 16:13-19

Scripture:
"I will give to you the keys of the kingdom of heaven. Whatever you bind on earth shall be bound in heaven; and whatever you loose on earth shall be loosed in heaven." (Matt 16:19)

Reflection: People who have keys have power. Be it keys to the school, the car, the office building, or to the kingdom of heaven, those who possess keys can enter and can exercise authority.

When Simon Peter professed faith in Jesus as the Messiah, a profession flowing from revelation and not from acquired knowledge, the Lord responded by entrusting to Peter the governance of the church. By being given the keys to the kingdom, Peter was assuming immense responsibility. God's flock must be tended well.

On this feast of the Chair of Peter, we have the opportunity to reflect upon the role of leadership. That leadership, if patterned after Jesus, must be one of service. Jesus came not to be served but to serve. And anyone selected, as Peter was, or elected, in the current dispensation, must exercise authority in being for others.

Giving the church "a shepherd's care" will also mean embracing the sufferings of Christ so as to participate in his glory. People in high office must be willing to embrace the sorrows and joys of the people. There must be no separation from the common lot of humanity. There must be no attempted exemption from the struggles to grow into the full stature of Christ.

Jesus came so that all might be one with the Father. The person who sits in the chair of Peter must have unity as the primary vision: unity with God and unity among all nations. The keys of the kingdom are given so that the power of God's love and mercy might be offered to all.

Questions: When you think of the Chair of Peter, do you think of servant leadership? What keys have been entrusted to you that foster unity and oneness in your situation? From your knowledge of church history, what pope emulated the Lord most clearly?

Prayer: Gracious God, you entrusted to frail, weak human beings the mission of the kingdom. Bless all those in leadership. Give them the wisdom and courage to fulfill your dream that all may be one.

March 19: Joseph, Husband of the Blessed Virgin

An Upright Man

Readings: 2 Sam 7:4-5a, 12-14a, 16; Rom 4:13, 16-18, 22; Matt 1:16, 18-21, 24a

Scripture:
"Joseph, son of David, do not be afraid to take Mary your wife into your home. For it is through the holy Spirit that this child has been conceived in her." (Matt 1:20b)

Reflection: God speaks to us in many ways: Sacred Scripture, the events of everyday life, the teachings of the wise, the stirrings of the heart, and, yes, even dreams. In a variety of ways God is guiding us in the ways of love, compassion, and forgiveness.

It was in sleep that God came to Joseph. Only after waking did Joseph, the upright and just man, put into action the message received. He would take Mary into his home and into his heart.

Together they would raise the child Jesus as he grew in age and wisdom. All of this despite fear and not knowing. It was trust and faith that empowered this good man to do God's will.

In our second reading for this great feast, St. Paul tells us of Abraham's faith and hope. Abraham trusted in the promise given to him despite its seeming implausibility. Saint Paul concludes this passage by saying that Abraham's faith was credited to him as justice. Is this not exactly what happened in Joseph's life? The implausibility, the trust, the faith, the hope! And yes, the justice! We honor today a faithful, just, and good man who was loyal to his lineage of being of the house of David.

In addition to Scripture, the teachings of the church, the happenings of everyday life, dreams, and intuitions, God also speaks to us through the lives of the saints. In them we witness faith, justice, and love. Today we see in Joseph a person who believed that what God said to him would be fulfilled. In Joseph, we see a person of justice, protecting the dignity of Mary in a culture that would reject her because of pregnancy. This son of David and husband of Mary was one who loved and sacrificed himself for his family. Our challenge is to emulate these qualities. We can do so through God's grace and the intercession of the saints.

Questions: How does God speak to you? In what sense are we all called to the same vocation that Joseph had: to be agents of love and justice in our times? What do you understand in Joseph being called an upright man?

Prayer: St. Joseph, from your place in heaven, intercede for us. Sometimes our faith is weak or almost nonexistent. Sometimes our love is shallow and paltry. Sometimes we fail in justice and uprightness. With Mary's assistance, we ask the Lord to send graces that will help us be true followers of the Lord Jesus.

March 25:
Annunciation of the Lord

The Kinswoman Elizabeth

Readings: Isa 7:10-14; 8:10; Heb 10:4-10; Luke 1:26-38

Scripture:
"And behold, Elizabeth, your relative, has also conceived a son in her old age, and this is the sixth month for her who was called barren; for nothing will be impossible for God." (Luke 1:36-37)

Reflection: A biography of Elizabeth, Mary's kinswoman, would be of few pages. We know so little of this woman and yet what we know is of great significance. In understanding but one aspect of Elizabeth's life, we gain insight into the feast of the Annunciation of our Lord.

Elizabeth was a wife and a mother. Her husband Zechariah struggled with the announcement of new life in the womb of his wife. She who was barren was now with child. Old Zechariah found this too difficult to believe and we know what happened to him. By contrast, Mary, though puzzled and afraid, embraced the message of the angel as the word of God. Everything was possible for those who believe.

Elizabeth's son John was like his mother in taking on the mission of giving life. His vocation as a prophet was to announce the good news of God's reign and to call the people to repentance. He became an announcer of freedom through the forgiveness of sin. Elizabeth experienced that freedom when, in the naming of her son, Zechariah was freed to once again speak. One can almost hear under Zechariah's breath: "Let it be done to me as you say."

Elizabeth had insight. When Mary came to her in the hill country of Judah, Elizabeth shouts out that Mary is full of grace. Elizabeth confirmed the message of the angel Gabriel. Mary hears again that she is blessed among women. Indeed, the Lord was with her, in her. Elizabeth saw grace, for both she and Mary had been loved since the beginning of time.

For those who have faith, nothing is impossible with God. Elizabeth, Mary's kinswoman and friend, believed, and history was changed forever.

Questions: How deep is your faith? In what ways are you sent to announce the good news of God's love and mercy in Jesus? Is the prayer—"I have come to do your will, O God"—a part of your spiritual journey?

Prayer: Lord Jesus, on this feast of your annunciation, we witness the faith of Mary and Elizabeth. Strong women they were and full of grace. Deepen our faith in you; strengthen our hope; increase our charity. We truly believe that nothing is impossible for you.

References

Dale, Jonathan. *Beyond the Spirit of the Age*. London: Quaker Home Service, 1996 (p. 8).

Herman, Brigid E. *Creative Prayer*. Brewster, MA: Paraclete Press, 1998 (p. 8).

Heschel, Abraham. *Man's Quest for God*. New York: Scribner's Sons, 1954 (p. 113).

Ker, Ian. *John Henry Newman: A Biography*. New York: Oxford University Press, 1988 (p. 113).

Lewis, C. S. *Mere Christianity*. New York: Macmillan Publishing Co., Inc., 1974 (p. 48).

O'Connor, Flannery *The Habit of Being*. New York: Farrar, Straus, Giroux, 1979 (p. 79).

Remnick, David. *Lenin's Tomb: The Last Days of the Soviet Empire*. New York: Vintage Books, 1994 (p. 241).

Schimel, Solomon. *Wounds Not Healed by Time: The Power of Repentance and Forgiveness*. New York: Oxford University Press, 2002 (p. 7).

Scott-Maxwell, Florida. *The Measure of My Days*. New York: Penguin Books, 1968 (p. 84).